SHE GOT THE BIGGEST ROOM

SHE GOT THE KIND OF BRACES THAT GO
ON THE *IN*SIDE OF YOUR TEETH

SHE GOT A DATE WITH BART JOCKSTRAP
EVEN THOUGH *YOU* SAW HIM FIRST

ISN'T IT TIME SHE GOT WHAT'S COMING TO HER?

10 WAYS TO DRIVE YOUR ADULT SISTER CRAZY

1. Marry a man she can't stand.

2. Lose weight.

3. Borrow the family heirlooms (silverware, diamond necklace, grandmother's tablecloth), then keep them.

4. Brag about your great sex life.

5. Lend her your copy of "The Demon Seed." Explain that she should consider it a "self-help" book.

6. Wear expensives shoes.

7. Blame her for everything. ("She hit me first . . . therefore, I can't find a decent job.")

8. Ask her if she has ever seen her birth certificate. Then ask if she needs help searching for her *real* family.

9. Get a big promotion at work and make her take you out to celebrate.

10. If all else fails tell her: "You're just like Mom."

LINDA SUNSHINE is the author of eight books including *WOMEN WHO DATE TOO MUCH* and *The New York Times* bestseller, *PLAIN JANE WORKS OUT*. She is currently on speaking terms with her sister, Susan, who is married to a dentist and has a very nice house in the suburbs.

Other books by Linda Sunshine

Fiction:

Women Who Date Too Much (And Those Who Should
  Be So Lucky)
Victoria's Book of Days
The Memoirs of Bambi Goldbloom: Or,
  Growing Up in New Jersey
Plain Jane's Thrill of Very Fattening Foods Cookbook
Plain Jane Works Out
Constant Stranger

Nonfiction (with John W. Wright):

The Best Hospitals in America
The 100 Best Rehabilitation Centers for Alcohol and
  Drug Abuse

"MOM LOVES ME BEST" (AND OTHER LIES YOU TOLD YOUR SISTER)

LINDA SUNSHINE

A PLUME BOOK

PLUME
Published by the Penguin Group
Penguin Books USA Inc., 375 Hudson Street,
New York, New York 10014, U.S.A.
Penguin Books Ltd, 27 Wrights Lane,
London W8 5TZ, England
Penguin Books Australia Ltd, Ringwood,
Victoria, Australia
Penguin Books Canada Ltd, 2801 John Street,
Markham, Ontario, Canada L3R 1B4
Penguin Books (N.Z.) Ltd, 182-190 Wairau Road,
Auckland 10, New Zealand

Penguin Books Ltd, Registered Offices:
Harmondsworth, Middlesex, England

First published by Plume, an imprint of New American library, a division of
Penguin Books USA Inc.

First Printing, July, 1990
10 9 8 7 6 5 4 3 2 1

The author gratefully acknowledges the following permissions:

Illustrations from ''The Impatient Heart'' first appeared in the Feb/March, 1955
issue of *Secret Hearts*, a trademark of DC Comics Inc. Copyright © 1954, 1982 DC
Comics Inc. All Rights Reserved. Originally published by Beverly Publishing
Company.

Written with Michaele Weissman, the chapter entitled ''Why Your Sister's Grass Is
Always Greener'' appeared in a somewhat different form as ''Wishful Thinkers'' in
the February, 1989 issue of *Special Reports*, Copyright © 1989 by Whittle Commu-
nications. Reprinted with permission. And many thanks to Michaele!

''Wedding Bell Blues'' also appeared in a different form in the August, 1989 issue
of *Woman*.

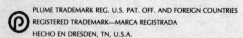

PLUME TRADEMARK REG. U.S. PAT. OFF. AND FOREIGN COUNTRIES
REGISTERED TRADEMARK—MARCA REGISTRADA
HECHO EN DRESDEN, TN, U.S.A.

PRINTED IN THE UNITED STATES OF AMERICA
Set in Optima
Designed by Leonard Telesca

I dedicate this book to my sister, Susan, with love . . . and to the dear friends in my life who are like sisters: Lena Tabori, Jean Holabird, Ella Stewart, Lee Halloway, Amanda Diaz, Stephie Sunshine, Lynnie Zeemont, Nan Diamond, Natasha and Katrina Fried.

And to my uncle, Bernie Deutsch, for 5,000 reasons.

CONTENTS

INTRODUCTION
MEET MY
SISTER, SUSAN

The Flanders Sisters. . . . were like Night and Day. Actually, they were more like 2 o'clock and 4 o'clock.

—Roz Chast
Parallel Views

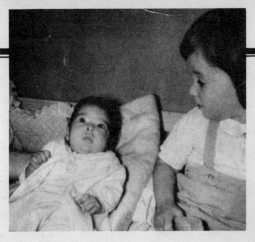

I am writing this book for my sister, Susan, whom I love dearly, even though I told her to drop dead often enough when we were kids.

I was eighteen months old when Susan was born, and to be truthful, I don't think I've ever quite forgiven her for upstaging my solo act.

As kids, we shared a bedroom and, afraid of the dark, invented games to ward off sleep. One game, which we played every night, was called "I'm sleeping." When one of us was too tired to talk any more, she would call out, "I'm sleeping." The other would reply, "I'm sleeping." Then, in unison, we'd both sing out, "We're all sleeping!" Okay, so it wasn't the most intellectually stimulating game, but it does point out one of the best features of having a sister: She makes you feel less alone.

It seems as though we were always together as young children. I remember the hours we spent, side by side, with our coloring books and 144 Crayolas. While we both loved to color, we had very different techniques.

I had a particular method that involved shading a border inside the black lines in a color just slightly darker than the filler space. I considered this very artistic.

My sister, ever more patient, was a total perfectionist (she still is!) and, thus, more meticulous about her coloring than me. It was always something of a crisis when she would go out of the lines. Usually, if this happened (say, when I, *by accident*, knocked her arm while she colored a delicate

3

curve), she would throw down the book and refuse to finish the picture. "It's ruined," she would wail, "why bother finishing it?"

So, then we would get out the comics. Romance comics were our absolute favorites. We liked to read them out loud. We fought over who got to be the beautiful heroine and who got stuck with the boy parts. My favorite parts, though, were the sound effects. For instance, when the heroine tossed her engagement ring into the river, the lake, the ocean, or any other available body of water (a regular plot twist in the romance genre), someone would be obliged to read: "Kerrrr-plunk." This was my all-time best sound effect; one which I can recreate today, upon request.

One Christmas, we got a portable tape recorder for a present, and I'm embarrassed to admit, we recorded our voices (sound effects and all) and then played it back, which made us laugh until we rolled off the bed.

Reading was always a favorite pastime in our house and comics were eventually replaced with real books. Always, one of us wanted to read the exact book that the other had just started. (See the chapter on Sibling Rivalry.)

One of our earliest books was *Little Women*. I read it first. Before passing it along to my sister, I happened to mention, "Beth dies!"

I liked to tell Susan the ending to the books I read before her. The angrier she got, the more I liked it.

So, I'd say, "I'm only kidding," and leave her to wonder whether I was lying when I told her Beth died, or whether I was lying when I told her I was kidding. This was my way of keeping my sister on her toes.

When I was in fourth grade and Susan was a baby third-grader, we moved from our apartment into a house in the suburbs. Our lives changed dramatically. We got our own bedrooms and learned about territorial imperatives.

And so, the real fighting started. I was older, wiser, and more mature than Susan and, almost always, instigated the fights. I deeply resented having to take care of my little sister when my parents went out for the evening, and to get back at Mom, I beat up Susan.

My favorite torture was to drag her across the floor of our finished basement—by her hair. She hated this a lot. Even more, she hated when I would pin her down and spit in her face.

I thought she fully deserved such treatment because she got on my nerves.

There was lots of other stuff that annoyed me. I got good grades in elementary school, mainly to impress my dad. Because of such achievements as making Honor Roll in seventh grade, I got labeled The Brains of the family, a role I came to sorely regret. Susan got labeled The Pretty One. For this I wanted to strangle her. Can you blame me? Given the choice, what pre-adolescent girl wants to be smart instead of pretty?

When Susan graduated from college, a year after I did, she moved into my apartment on the east side of New York. She stayed for a year while trying to decide whether or not to marry her college boyfriend. One night we started talking about our childhood. "You know," she said, "I always envied the way you talked back to your teachers."

"What?" I was incredulous, never imagining my sister envied anything about me. "You envied me for that? I envied the way you looked in a two-piece."

For most of the evening—and well into the early morning —we revealed the things we'd always envied in each other.

While we'd been sisters all our lives, it wasn't until that night that we became friends.

We still fight now and then. Of course, I no longer drag her across the floor or try to spit in her face, although sometimes I say things to her that are not very nice. And she forgives me.

Despite the cracks I make about Susan in this book, I know I got really lucky in the sister department.

Here's a sister-secret we've never shared with anyone.

Once, in the heat of a ferocious adolescent fight, I kicked my sister so hard that I broke her finger. (It was an accident, I wanted to break her face.) Yet, instead of ratting on me, she told Mom she'd walked into a door.

How could you not love a sister like that?

HOW I
RESEARCHED
THIS BOOK

This book will most certainly be hailed as a landmark work in the study of sibling relationships. That's because almost nothing else has been written on the subject.

My aim in writing this book was to present the latest thinking, the most up-to-date research, any available psychological data, long buried information, and historical perspectives; all combined with my own personal, highly biased, and subjective opinions. In short, I wanted to put together a ground-breaking, compellingly written volume that would sell like hotcakes.

In order to gather the latest thinking on the controversial subject of sibling relationships, I devoted long hours to the public library. However since, as I said, little has been written on the subject, most of my time was spent writing long lists of things I wanted to buy with the advance money my publisher put up for this book, napping, and, occasionally, playing with the new computers recently installed on the third floor of the library. My intellectual stimulation came from trying to solve the daily crossword puzzle in the newspaper.

For lack of anything else to read, I began investigating my theories about sibling relationships by reading Nora Ephron, Delia Ephron, Amy Ephron, and Efrem Zimbalist, Jr. I felt on familiar territory, not far from *77 Sunset Strip*, and was encouraged to persuade my own sister to also write a book. I read the Brontë sisters and their modern counterparts, the Collins sisters. I went back to the romance comics of my youth. I re-read *The Bad Seed*, which I once thought was based on my sister's life. Mostly though, I flipped through *People* and prayed for lunchtime.

In addition to library research and reading, my information base was supplemented by extensive interviewing. Since I am basically a shy person and do not feel comfortable approaching strangers, I decided to limit my interviews to my close personal friends, asking everyone I knew embarrassing questions about their siblings.

Most of my friends and acquaintances were unwilling to talk until I either revealed personal details of my relationship with my sister or the intimate details of my sister's relationship with her husband which she told me in the strictest confidence. (Sorry, Sis, but this is for publication!)

As a last resort, when all else failed to win over an unwilling subject, I offered cash.

In most cases, the cash worked best and I was able to garner enough material to make this book appear to cover a wide spectrum of different individuals. In truth, though, almost all my case studies come from people of the same social class, ethnic origin, and life experience. We're all pretty much the same age, too—although I am a good six months younger than most of my friends, except for Janis C. who's still in her late twenties (but don't hate her too much, she's at least thirty pounds overweight). I suppose I should add that almost every case history cited within this text is highly exaggerated.

I solicited diaries and letters from my case studies. I claimed I needed such data as additional pieces of evidence, but really, I wanted to read the stuff because I'm just plain nosy and love to poke around in other people's personal belongings.

I followed leads whenever I could find them—which was almost never.

I taped all the conversations I had with my case studies so that I could quote accurately, but then unfortunately, I discovered I'd forgotten to put batteries in the tape recorder so I came away with nothing but blank tapes and lots of wasted

energy spent punching buttons and carrying around exten-
sion cords. (I'm no mechanical genius, that's for sure.)

I tried to conduct most of my interviews in my subject's
home so that I could make a first-hand evaluation of where
and how they lived. Also, it saved me a bundle in restaurant
bills. Most of the time, I got offered a cup of coffee or a
drink—if not an invitation to dinner—from my subjects. For
this reason, I highly recommend this interviewing procedure
to my fellow colleagues.

I preserved the anonymity of everyone who participated in
my research mainly so that no one could sue me after
publication.

To expand the range of my raw data, I attempted to
include repeated interviews over the course of several months
with my subjects. However, as happens even among the
best of friends (and certainly among sisters), I often fought
with my subjects and stopped talking to them for extended
periods of time. This made interviewing difficult, if not
impossible. It was at this point in my research that I
decided, as a way of saving energy for both myself and my
subjects, to fabricate most of my case studies. This method
proved extremely time-saving, and because I didn't have
to schedule interview times, I got to watch my daytime
soaps.

I also made up quotes whenever it suited my purpose.

My objective was not so much accuracy as completion.
The manuscript was due in eight weeks.

I discovered that once I gave up trying to be factual about
every little point of reference, I was able to whiz through the
manuscript in less than two weeks—although to my own
credit I should add that *twice* I worked on weekends. Once,
I even worked on Saturday night. (Top that, Miss Diane
Sawyer, or, excuse me, should I say—Mrs. Mike Nichols!)

By finishing so quickly, I had a good six weeks to proof-
read and polish the final draft of my manuscript. Instead, I
decided to visit friends in Los Angeles where—I'm thrilled to
report—I spotted George Hamilton in the parking lot of the

Beverly Hills Hotel. (By the way, he *is* the most suntanned man in Hollywood—you can tell your friends I said so!)

I should add that, in case you're wondering, my qualifications to write a book about sisters are twofold. First, I have a sister, and second, I was pretty desperate for the advance money. I need not explain my financial difficulties to anyone living above their means in the 1990s.

As for my sister, you'll meet her in the next chapter. I hope she'll be a good sport about this book. If not, I'm telling Mom.

TAKE THIS TEST: ARE YOU A GOOD SISTER, OR WHAT?

> Never praise a sister to a sister, in the hope of your compliment ever reaching the proper ears.
> —Rudyard Kipling
> *Plain Tales from the Hills*, 1888

We begin this book with a pop test, just like your worst days in high school. The reason for this test is simple. Because you have known your sister for a very long time, it is often difficult to see her as she truly exists in real life. Women often have romantic, unrealistic notions about their sisters. You still see your sibling as a child. Psychiatrists call this Frozen Misconceptions (a real term that I didn't make up). It is sometimes a shock to realize that your sister is an adult, with a life of her own, and that she no longer depends on you to tell her what she thinks. (Although she could probably use your advice about her clothes.)

At almost any age, it is difficult, if not impossible, to avoid conflict with your sister. Many things about her may drive you up a wall, especially because she represents so much of what you can't stand about yourself.

The following test will be helpful in allowing you to focus on the areas of conflict you may have with your sister. Try to answer as openly and honestly as possible. Do not look up the answers at the end of the test before completing each and every question. And keep your eyes to yourself!

1) Overall, how do you rate your relationship with your sister:
   a) good
   b) bad
   c) indifferent

2) Are you threatened by your sister's:
   a) accomplishments
   b) failures
   c) inner thighs

3) Would you define your relationship with your sister as:
   a) equal
   b) one of you is the leader, the other follows
   c) she gets all the good stuff

4) Expressing emotion is:
   a) easy for her, hard for me
   b) hard for me, easy for her
   c) not considered polite in our family

5) Do you encourage your sister's involvement in new interests or activities?
   a) yes
   b) no
   c) only if there's something in it for me

6) If you answered a) or c) to the above, what method do you use to encourage your sister in new activities:
   a) by talking to her
   b) by getting involved in the activity with her
   c) kicking, biting, and scratching

7) How often do you compare yourself with your sister:
   a) hardly ever
   b) occasionally
   c) whenever Mom calls

8) What activities do you enjoy doing with your sister?
   a) exercising
   b) shopping
   c) borrowing money

9) Are you influenced by your sister's opinion?
   a) yes
   b) no
   c) only when she agrees with me

10) In what areas do you compete with your sister?
   a) in our social lives
   b) in our professional lives
   c) in our mother's kitchen

11) How often do you see your sister?
   a) at least once a week
   b) at every major holiday
   c) at every family funeral

12) How often do you fight with your sister?
   a) hardly ever
   b) all the time
   c) only when she's a bitch

13) When do you seek your sister's advice?
   a) hardly ever
   b) all the time
   c) whenever my therapist permits

14) How do you deal with a point of conflict with your sister?
   a) confront it
   b) ignore it
   c) kicking, biting, and scratching

15) Which of you is more likely to compromise or apologize?
   a) your sister
   b) you
   c) none of the above

16) What would happen if you ever shared your true feelings with your sister?
   a) she'd cry
   b) we'd feel closer to each other
   c) I'd be in a cast

17) What is the most positive aspect of your relationship with your sister?
   a) companionship
   b) love
   c) her country house

18) If your sister had only one week to live, what would you want to tell her?
   a) you love her
   b) you'll miss her
   c) you lied about her being adopted

19) The things you like best about your sister:
   a) her personality
   b) her honesty
   c) her shoes

20) The things your sister likes best about you:
   a) your personality
   b) your honesty
   c) your shoes

SCORE: If you answered a) to the majority of questions you are a Big Liar, Young Lady. Go to your room, and while you're there, clean out that closet of yours!

If you answered b) to most of these questions then you are semi—well adjusted and seem to have a decent relationship with your sister. Overall, you are a good, if boring, sibling.

If you answered c) to most of the questions in this test you get a gold star for honesty but a black mark for being so obnoxious. You would do well to apologize to your sister for being such a pain in the neck and, while you're at it, return the clothes you borrowed from her.

HISTORY, SOCIOLOGY, AND OTHER BACKGROUND STUFF

Molly, my sister and I fell out,
  And what do you think it was all about?
She loved coffee and I loved tea,
And that was the reason we couldn't agree.
                              —Nursery Rhyme

In the beginning was your mother. And your mother spoke the words. And the words were these: "Sisters who love each other do not fight."

And the words were wrong. (Sorry, Mom!)

The truth is: Sisters who love each other fight all the time.

If you don't understand how a woman could both love her sister dearly and want to wring her neck at the same time, then you were probably an only child.

Ancient History

Great sister combos have appeared throughout history, dating all the way back to ancient Greek mythology when, on Mount Olympus, there were two lovely bands of sisters, the Muses and the Graces. In *Mythology*, renowned author Edith Hamilton writes extensively about the Muses and the Graces and I was going to research the subject but Ms. Hamilton's book was checked out of the library on the day I thought of it. (Good for Ms. Hamilton!)

Anyway, if I start this book all the way back there, it will take forever and a day to get to modern times, so let's just flash ahead several thousand years to the 1960s, a decade I can really relate to.

Modern Trends in Sibling Relationships, Seriously

Several of today's societal and sociological trends have greatly affected sibling relationships. Among these trends are family size, average life span, working mothers, family mobility, and divorce rates. I know that all of these trends are accurate because each and every one has been discussed by both Phil Donahue and Geraldo.

We first notice, since the time of ancient Greek mythology and last Tuesday, that family size has shrunk significantly. Mom and Dad probably came from a much larger family than yours. They may have had three or four siblings. And your grandparents probably came from an even bigger family. Why, only sixty, seventy, or one hundred years ago (I forgot which number is most accurate), families with twelve or thirteen siblings were not at all uncommon.

In our current society, family size is infinitely smaller, due mainly to the cost of Nike sneakers. Today, most families consist of no more than two children and we can all thank heavens for that. Can you imagine sharing the bathroom with *eleven* other sisters? Who knows when you'd get your shot at the hot rollers?

Our families are not only smaller, but family members tend to live much longer. In 1900, the average American lived to the age of 47; today, our average life span has increased to the age of 74 for men. Most women live well into their eighties. This means that life with a sibling can last sixty to *eighty* years! Think about that the next time you are fighting with your sister. Remember she's the one person in your entire life who will see you from high chair to wheelchair.

Over the past few decades, the increased number of working mothers has also had a tremendous effect on sibling relationships. Required more and more to babysit, siblings are spending more time with each other, unsupervised by

Mommy. Oh sure, they may have a day-care worker or baby-sitter looking after them, but it is generally acknowledged that when not monitored by a PCA (Personally Committed Adult), children tend to spend more time with their hands in the cookie jar and their fingers on the X-rated video cassettes.

Working mothers have also had a dramatic effect on one of the most important and influential aspects of childhood development: that is, television programming. Stay-at-home ideal moms like June Cleaver and Donna Reed have been replaced with working moms like Clare Huxtable and Rose-anne. No wonder more moms than ever are working—Susan Saint James and Elyse Keaton sure have nicer clothes (and better shoes) than Mrs. Ozzie Nelson.

Working moms and dads travel more than ever these days resulting in Increased Family Mobility. This is a fancy way of saying that, today, it's more likely than ever that you and the family have moved several times during the course of your childhood. Dad or Mom gets offered a big new job in another part of the country and you all pack up and move.

Changing schools and friends is hard on children and can often make them desperate and lonely enough to form closer ties with a sibling. Children caught in this predicament should be advised not to panic. Parents need to remind their children that, eventually, they will meet someone in school who'll relieve them of the burden of being nice to their sister.

Divorce rates, single parent families, and remarriages have changed the way that families develop and relate to each other. Younger children may have a difficult time adjusting when parents divorce and remarry, especially when new children from previous marriages are brought into the family. This phenomenon has created a whole new genre in the family structure: the step-sibling, or step-sib for short. Of course, children do feel better once they realize the advantage of living with stepsibs: You are given the opportunity of teasing and taunting someone not of your own blood, in the comfort of your very own home.

For older children, divorce can be doubly traumatic after Dad moves out and Mom starts dating again, especially if she has more dates than her children.

Psychological Factors: Stress and Anxiety

Sociologists have noted that the twin components of life in the last part of the twentieth century are stress and anxiety. Previously, it was thought that just because no one talked about anxiety until the latter part of the 1970s, it never before existed.

Recent discoveries, however, point out that anxiety has been around for over one hundred years, and was mentioned by Freud as early as 1870 when he wrote in his diary: "I have a date tonight with Greta, the blonde who sits behind me in geography. Boy! Am I anxious!"

Stress, of course, is a comparatively new syndrome and was first reported in 1969, when Richard Nixon was elected President.

You're Only Jung Once

Carl Jung, a shrink who became almost as famous as Freud (but not quite), used the word "persona" to describe the mask one creates to hide behind. To protect ourselves, we only let people see our outward masks. Some of us create better masks than others. For instance, give Cher and Jane Fonda both an A+ and Leona Helmsley a C–/D+. Jung claimed that everyone—not just movie stars and convicted millionaires—had a publicly presented self. For regular folks, your "persona" is the person known to your parents, aunts and uncles, grandparents, babysitters, and guidance counselors.

At an early age, children develop a "persona" that is acceptable to the authority figures in his or her life. Kids can often be very effective at putting on a good show for their parents. Mom and Dad may think you're a little angel and never suspect you're stealing money from Mom's purse whenever she's not looking.

Your sister, on the other hand, *knows everything!*

While you can hide your true self from Mom and Dad, your sister knows the core of you. She sees you being mean to the family dog; she hears you lying to your best friend; she knows when you've cheated on your chemistry paper. More than Santa Claus, your sister knows when you've been bad and good. She can peer into the deepest, darkest recesses of your personality and see how gross, inconsiderate, selfish, and just plain icky you really are. This, of course, is a terrifying prospect and one of the reasons you get so mad when your sister says, "Boy, you are really, really phony!"

Even though your "persona" negates your sister's opinion by calling her a stupid idiot, deep down, your real self agrees with her assessment.

With this kind of leverage, is it any wonder that sibling relationships are fraught with conflict? Or that sometimes you express the desire to have your sister shrivel up and disappear off the face of the earth?

Parents often mistake such attitudes for a lack of real feeling between their children. They believe that sisters who yell and scream at each other are expressing only animosity but this is not true.

It's an absolute given that sisters love each other. How could it be otherwise? Your sister is the only creature on earth who shares your heritage, history, environment, DNA, bone structure, and contempt for stupid Aunt Gertie.

Your sister is like your own heartbeat, she's a part of you that's easy to take for granted.

There are many special moments between sisters when they act particularly loving and generous toward each other. Say, on Christmas Eve when your sister buys you a really neat pair of rhinestone earrings or during that time she sat up all night holding your hand because Rocky Rissoto didn't ask you to the Senior Prom. But parents rarely see these times.

More often, sisters are at each other's throats. The real barometer, then, of their affection toward each other is how well they deal with the down side of sibling relationships: the rivalry, the fights, the jealousy, the petty grievances, the deep resentments, the competition, the sharing, and the urge to do bodily harm to the little demon who's stealing away all of Mommy's attention.

Given the nature of most sibling relationships, parents have often marveled that it's something of a miracle their children make it to adulthood without killing each other or, at the very least, poking out an eye.

Chronological Chart: Stages of Sibling Relationships from Pre-Birth to Adulthood

In the following chart, we show the five basic stages in the development of a typical sibling relationship. We define these stages as:

1) Pre-Birth
Encompasses the period before the arrival of a sibling. During this time, Mom carefully prepares you for the coming event, in the best tradition of Dr. Spock (the baby doctor, not the director of *Three Men and a Baby*). She talks about how you are about to get a friend for life. She predicts that family life is about to change radically, but as far as you (the child) are concerned, all that really happens is that Mom gets very fat.

2) Post-Birth
Mom disappears for a day or two, although to you (the child) a day or two feels like five years. Daddy tells you how happy everyone is but your main concern is: Who will cook your breakfast in the morning?

When Mom does finally return, she is carrying a tiny bundle, your sibling. You are happy—for about five minutes. As far as you can tell, this prune-faced not-yet-a-person does nothing but spit up and howl all night. You are amazed that your parents want to keep it in the house.

3) Middle Childhood

A relatively uneventful period—before your sibling begins walking or talking—when you live with the illusion that your relationship with your kid sister will never change. She's not so bad, you think.

4) Mid-Childhood Crisis

The arguments begin. You fight about property, clothes, friends, personal rights, school, and the world in general, but still, you see your childhood as unending and unchanging.

5) Adolescence

Everything changes. Your body, clothes, sense of humor, taste in music, hair, fingernails. You can no longer talk or play with your sibling.

This causes a great deal of friction in the family as everyone fights for control of the family thermostat. Since no one can ever win such battles, your emotional thermometer now has only two settings: Arctic ice and nuclear meltdown.

6) Adulthood

You leave the house, move on with your life—marry, move in with someone, whatever. You work, have kids of your own, whatever. You recall your childhood as golden. You are trapped with what psychologists call Frozen Misconceptions. You only remember the idyllic times of middle childhood.

These stages can best be understood by the kind of language one uses during these phases, as exemplified in the following chart:

PRE-BIRTH   "Why can't I have a baby
                             sister?"

POST-BIRTH   "Do we have to keep her?"
                             "No fair!"

MIDDLE CHILDHOOD	"Let's play Patty-cake!" "Here's how to use the remote." "Can I have some of your Twinkie?"
MID-CHILDHOOD CRISIS	"I'm Mommy's favorite." "You weren't alive then." "You were an accident." "There's no Santa Claus."[1] "I'm telling." "Do over!" "Stop repeating me." "STOP REPEATING ME!!!"
ADOLESCENCE	"Your best friend is fat." "You're fat." "I'm telling!" "Mom and Dad are doing IT!" "I'M TELLING!" "Get out of my closet!" "You let her get away with murder!" "You *always* take her side!"
ADULTHOOD	"You're majoring in WHAT?" "Your boyfriend is a jerk." "Looks more like a half carat to me." "Of course I'll be your maid of honor." "Why can't I have a baby niece?"

[1]Alternatives: Easter Rabbit, Peter Pan, Pot of Gold, more jelly doughnuts.

INFANCY: BABY SISTERS

A baby sister is nicer than a goat.
You'll get used to her.
—Lynn Alpern and Esther Blumenfeld
Oh, Lord, I Sound Just Like Mama

The Birth Order Principle

Experts have recently determined that where you were born in the family structure is critical to your development. Your B.O. (that's Birth Order) determines whether you turn out to be Mom's Beloved First Born or Eleanor's cry-baby sister. You either get to assemble the new bike with Daddy or play checkers with only nine pieces and a button. As a sister, you will soon learn that life isn't always fair and that nobody gets all the Mallomars for herself.

There are three basic positions in the Birth Order Principle: Eldest, Middle, and Baby. With each additional child, the cycle repeats itself because Mom and Dad are too tired, by then, to invent new methods for childrearing.

Each position has its relative advantages and drawbacks. A brief explanation follows:

The First Born

For as long as you were an Only Child, life was bliss. You had everything you could possibly want for happiness, only you did not know it. You assumed this was the way life worked. Like Adam and Eve in the Garden of Eden, you learned—too late—that ignorance is better than learning how to share.

If a sibling did not appear before you learned to talk, your first sentence was probably. "Why can't I have a baby sister to play with?" This was the first major mistake of your life. All that Only Child attention made you overly generous and heady with power.

Here's what usually happens:

A few months before baby sister arrives, Mommy makes a concerted effort to make you feel even more snug and secure. She often talks to you about how much she loves you and how much fun you'll all have when "the baby" arrives. She assures you that "the baby" will not detract from her time with you. This, of course, is a whopping big lie.

Once baby sister arrives, you discover that Mommy is too busy to sing "Itsy Bitsy Spider" with you and that Daddy is too tired to play horsey.

You discover you are the only level-headed family member who does not go bananas whenever raisin-face sucks her toes.

You begin to realize you've made a horrible mistake. "Take her back!" you scream. "I changed my mind."

And, for the first time in your short life, Mommy and Daddy actually *refuse* to fulfill your request. This is when you fully grasp the concept of nonreturnable.

It will take some time, several years in fact, but eventually, you will come around to seeing that there are some advantages to having the snot-nose around, particularly when you are homesick or it's raining outside.

Baby sister almost always lets you select the board games, especially after you threaten to lock her in the basement and turn out the lights.

Usually, you can con your sister into selling you Boardwalk, dirt cheap. Or, she lets you make up card games with elaborate rules that you can change if she starts to win.

She helps you color in the big spaces.

You always have someone to blame for the mud tracks on the floor, the mess in the sink, or the spinach on the ceiling.

You do mean things to her and she doesn't tell Mommy.

She lets you borrow all her stuff.

She asks *you* questions, instead of Mommy.

She takes out the garbage, when it's really your turn, in exchange for a promise not to leave her alone when Mommy and Daddy go out at night.

She thinks you are worldly, knowledgeable, cool.

After a while, you come to appreciate the ways in which your baby sister worships you. You begin to recapture some of the sense of power you felt as an Only Child.

Unfortunately, she grows out of this by the age of seven, leading you to conclude that sisters are okay as long as they remain gullible and stupid.

The Second Born

Being the second-born child, you do not know what life was like *without* your sister. She has been around since the day you were born and is as much a part of your life as the mobile hanging over your crib.

There are many obvious advantages to being the youngest child.

You are the cutest.

Your sister makes you feel more secure. When Mommy and Daddy argue, your sister holds your hand and tells you not to worry. She protects you because she is braver than you.

You often feel that it is you and your sister against the world.

You always have someone around who is tall enough to reach the Ding-Dongs.

You fantasize that when you are grown-up, your sister will fix you up with cute boys. (You are in for a rude awakening, but never mind.)

She is always there to teach you how to use Kotex, to explain the meaning of "French kiss" and "going all the way."

Inevitably, your sister's information is totally wrong but you will not discover this until you are twenty-seven years old.

Of course, there are also many disadvantages to being the youngest. The major drawback is that you will always be younger than your sister so she will always think she knows more than you.

Your sister's problems will seem much more crucial to your parents than yours.

Your sister will often hide in the closet just to scare you.

You will often be called bad names by your sister who will learn how to curse long before you do.

Despite all this, the real danger of being the youngest is that your lose your status in the event that another sibling enters the house. The fall from grace from being the youngest to the "middle" can cause a severe case of the bends.

The Middle

Have pity on the middle child for her lot in life is not an easy one. The Middle exists in a kind of vacuum. She does not get the pressure to perform like the First Born or the attention of the Baby. Basically, she is left to her own devices.

She spends most of her childhood grabbing at straws.

She will often rebel to attract attention.

While this is painful in childhood, it does allow for a certain independence in adolescence and adulthood. The Middle is pretty much free to do her own thing.

She will believe in outrageous haircuts and dress in rubber or leather. She will be willing to endure multiple ear piercings and, sometimes, tattooing very sensitive body parts.

She will often attend college on another coast.

When she marries, she will not have more than two children.

Her favorite cookies will be Oreos.

Why Sisters Fight: The Trickle Down Theory of Family Aggression

As a child, the first thing you remember is the fighting. Well, there's a good reason why there was so much yelling going on in your childhood. Psychologists call it the Trickle Down Theory of Family Aggression.

According to the principles of this theory:

Daddy yells at Mommy.
Mommy yells at her First Born.
The First Born pulls Middle's hair.
Middle pokes the Baby.
Baby kicks the dog.
Dog pees on the carpet.
Mommy yells at dog.
Daddy yells at Mommy.
(Repeat ad infinitum)

All I Really Need to Know I Learned from My Sister

My sister taught me everything I really need to know, and she was only in sixth grade at the time.

I kept a diary at the time, and I'm amazed by how well my sister's credo has weathered the test of adolescence and adulthood. She was so right on, in fact, that I never had to waste time inventing my own credo—I simply copied hers.

Here's my Sister's Credo:

Share everything with your sister but don't expect anything in return.

Play by my rules. They're fair, I promise.

Don't hit me or I'll tell.

Touch my things and you die.

Clean up after yourself and me.

Lend me money when I ask.

Buy me expensive birthday gifts.

Leave the house when I bring home a friend.

Goldfish and hamsters and grandparents all die some day. So will you. I'm living forever.

Remember the Dick and Jane books and how boring they seemed next to page 79 of *Peyton Place*.

When you go out into the world, bring me back a Tab.

MIDDLE CHILDHOOD

Smile and the world smiles with you.
Cry and you go to your room.

—My Mom

Sibling Rivalry

Sibling rivalry is one of the most basic, elemental aspects of having or being a sister. Sibling rivalry is a required condition of your siblinghood; this is not an elective course like, say, home economics. You simply cannot be living in the same house, with the same parents and a finite number of toys and Cheez Doodles, without incurring at least a minimal amount of kicking, biting, and scratching.

In attempting to define the term "sibling rivalry" psychologists turn first to the traditional dictionary definition of the term "rival," which comes from the Latin word *rivalis* meaning "having rights to the same stream." (I'm not really sure how to interpret this definition but I thought I'd pass it along as proof that I did my homework on the subject.)

According to noted child psychologist Dr. Margery Momsuch, a rival is "one of two or more striving to reach or obtain something only one can possess." Dr. Momsuch uses similar words to more specifically define a *sibling* rival as "one of two or more striving to reach or obtain the last Hershey bar that only one can possess."

While there are numerous case studies of sibling rivalry charted in almost every developmental age group from one-day-old to just-moments-before-death, scientists have recently discovered that the predisposition toward sibling rivalry begins even *before* birth. In a recent federally funded study, molecular biologists at the famed University of Shreveport were scrounging around in the DNA link one afternoon when they happened upon an actual living gene that causes sibling rivalry. They aptly named this gene The Squabble Factor.

Apparently, The Squabble Factor is transferred within the DNA of your parents. To use modern terminology, The Squabble Factor is faxed from Dad to Mom from the first contact between sperm and egg. It is part of your genetic make-up.

Genetic Make-Up

For those less scientifically minded (who probably cut Biology class every Tuesday to hang out and smoke cigarettes in the girls room), it should be explained that DNA is part of your genetic make-up and is every bit as important as your mascara, blusher, and eyebrow pencil. DNA is like a blueprint that determines the color of your eyes, the length of your legs, the shape of your earlobes, and the texture of your hair. If you are not particularly pleased with your looks, you should blame your DNA instead of your hairdresser or the blueberry pancakes you eat for breakfast every morning.

Simply put, every one of us possesses a gene predisposing us toward rivalry, competition, and fits of envy with any past, present, or future siblings.

The presence of The Squabble Factor is evidenced by many well-documented childhood symptoms. The gene causes young children to covet the front seat of all moving vehicles, hoard all the M&Ms, borrow clothes without asking permission, and tell lies to babysitters and substitute teachers. It is the gene that controls the voice box, enabling young children to whine in a high-pitched voice. Examples of The Squabble Factor can be found in such phrases as: "If she can stay up to watch TV, so can I!" and "Why does she always get the biggest piece of cake?" and the ever-popular "She makes me want to barf!"

The Squabble Factor enables children to develop their cursing skills at a remarkably early age and to remember a string of invectives, even if heard only once, uttered by a parent when the car broke down in the middle of a thunderstorm. It is also the gene that carries the basic tactics for combat fighting including such basics as hair-pulling, spit-ball accuracy, and under-the-dinner-table-shin-kicking.

A Classic Case of Sibling Rivalry

Sibling rivalry has a long history, dating back to the time of the brothers Grimm. One of the first recorded cases of traumatic sibling rivalry was that of Cinderella S., the youngest, prettiest, and thinnest of several girls in her family. Naturally, Cinderella caught hell for her looks from her older step-sisters and plump step-mom. Forced to clean out the fireplace and wear tattered hand-me-downs, Cinderella never got to visit the mall, wear Navajo jewelry, or test drive a Jeep. The poor thing never once stood in front of a dressing room mirror wearing a $750 Perry Ellis raw silk jacket.

Little wonder, then, that one day she rebelled. (Wouldn't you?) Borrowing a new dress and a souped-up pumpkin 325i, fearless Cinderella sneaked out of the house after dark to check out the ball at the local palace.

Like everyone's younger, prettier sister, Cinderella got to dance a lot and was asked out by the cutest, best dancer at the party—which only enraged her older sisters even more. Even her best friend Mabel was pissed off. "What's she got that's so hot?" Mabel asked her second-best friend, Adele.

"Great shoes," Adele replied.

Legend records that Cinderella, leaving early to make her midnight curfew, "accidentally" left behind one of her slippers, although, today, psychiatrists will tell us that there is no such thing as an accident.

Anyway, lucky, manipulative Cinderella was tracked down and found through that somewhat obscure piece of evidence (a business card would've been a lot easier on the Prince and everyone else in the kingdom). Unlike real life 1990s style, in the end, Cinderella got the Prince (not the one backed up by Revolution, but another one who was almost as rich and famous), the big house in the country, and lots of revenge on her mean and rotten older siblings, which only goes to clearly demonstrate the obvious moral of the story: It *always* pays to wear the right shoes.

Sibling Tussle

Although the term "sibling rivalry" has been around since Cinderella's time, noted child psychologist Dr. Margery Momsuch objects to the term as being too clinical and cold and prefers to use the phrase "sibling tussle." Explains Dr. Momsuch, "What really happens between siblings is that they squabble, make up, share their graham crackers, squabble over the last cookie, make up, share the potato chips, squabble over the last one, make up, etc., etc. Then they sit down at the dinner table and throw spaghetti at each other."

In her carefully chosen phrasing and astute observation, Dr. Momsuch points out the sensitive give and take, growth and testing that is a constant in the development of the sibling relationship. All this is deftly summed up in her landmark paper, *Siblings Are for Slugging*, where she notes that sibling tussles can be a valuable spur to the child's learning to live with others, win victories, suffer defeats, love, and cope with their own unloving feelings. "Through their sisters and brothers, children learn how the world works and they are better able to prepare themselves for life as frustrated housewives or, for boy children, as henpecked husbands. They also become well suited for a career in education or fast-food service."

In her work with children, the doctor is often hired to help children deal with troublesome sibling relationships. After many years of studying the ways in which children relate to their siblings, she has devised three general guidelines to better enable her patients to deal with feelings of aggression, spite, and just plain old meanness.

Children who visit Dr. Momsuch's clinic are given Xeroxed copies of her Three Little Rules. Younger children are supplied with the audio cassette version.

The Three Little Rules

- The first and most important rule is to always, always remember that acts of violence between siblings are absolutely forbidden when either parent is within earshot. "Take your battles to the basement, the laundry room, the attic, the garage, the closet, the walk-in refrigerator," advises the doctor, "anywhere where your parents will not see or hear you."

- If caught with your hands around your sibling's neck, your foot on her back, or your fist in her ribs, *deny, deny, deny* that you are causing pain for the little brat. Claim you are in the middle of teaching your kid sister the latest dance step or fall back on the "We're only horsing around" position.

- If caught without hope of escape, especially if a bloody nose or any broken bones are involved, DO NOT accept the responsibility. Plead your case with the Sibling Fifth Amendment: "But she started it!" and hang tough. Show fear or guilt to a parent and you're sure to get the book thrown at you.

Dr. Momsuch is particularly insistent that her patients adhere to The Three Little Rules and has often refused to treat patients she defines as Little Miss Goody Two Shoes. "A child who cannot learn to palm off responsibility to cover her ass is just not going to survive in the 1990s," claims this noted psychologist. "And I don't want to waste my valuable time on the incurables. I only want patients who will make enough use of my services so that they will grow up to be junk bond dealers or corporate lawyers and be able to pay their future shrink fees."

Favoritism

Nothing breeds sibling rivalry more than the dreaded disease of parental favoritism. After many centuries, favoritism is finally being recognized by psychologists as one of the most prominent yet cleverly concealed ailments of otherwise normal households.

Make no mistake. Favoritism is an insidious, difficult-to-diagnose disease that can go undetected for years. Parents are loathe to admit that they favor one child over the other. "I love both my children exactly the same," parents will insist. As any sibling will tell you, this is an excellent lie.

According to the latest statistics, the odds of any parent feeling equally about their children are 2,798 to 1.

The Denial of Favoritism

Because most parents refuse to acknowledge that they favor one child over another, favoritism has come to be known as a "disease of denial."

Children who grow up in an environment haunted by favoritism are at a loss to change the family situation that breeds such a disease. The victim, that is the child who is at the short end of the favoritism stick, is unlikely to be believed when she accuses her parents of suffering from the disease. Her cries of "You always let *her* get away with everything" are vehemently denied by the parent. The child is often punished for "being too sensitive" or "making mountains out of molehills," to use typical parental euphemisms. "It's not true," parents will say, "we treat you both the same. Now shut up and go to your room. We have to type your sister's term paper.''

On the other hand, the favored child develops a sense of superiority, power, and entitlement; for obvious reasons, she will do nothing to alter the family situation, unless she's a complete pinhead.

In refusing to admit that one child is favored over the other, parents make this disease even more difficult to diagnose. While the varieties of favoritism are endless, there are several clear-cut signs that children are victims of this parental disease. If you recognize any of the following symptoms, then your family may be suffering from favoritism.

Checklist

TELLTALE SIGNS OF FAVORITISM

	The Favored Child	The Victim
Nickname	☐ "Darling"	☐ "Numbskull"
Lunchbox	☐ Barbie black patent leather	☐ Brown bag
Lunch	☐ Thermos of chicken soup, a steak sandwich, a bag of chips, Jell-O pudding cup, apple juice	☐ Lean Cuisine (frozen)
Living Accommodations	☐ Your own room with CD player, private Princess phone	☐ Fold-out couch in living room
Transportation	☐ Suzuki 4-wheel drive	☐ Your own two feet
Vacations	☐ Switzerland	☐ Finished basement

Educational Tools	☐ Mac II, laser printer, modem, scanner	☐ Typewriter and Webster's
Curfew	☐ Before dawn	☐ 9:30 on the dot
College Education	☐ Anything Ivy League	☐ School of Hard Knocks
Saturday Activities	☐ Plays tennis with Mom at the club	☐ Cleans garage with family pet
Clothes	☐ Calvin Klein	☐ Goodwill
Allowance	☐ Checking account, American Express Gold Card	☐ $2.50/week, no credit
Haircuts	☐ Mr. Rudolph, at salon in the mall	☐ Dolores (cleaning lady), in the bathroom
After-School Activities	☐ Ballet lessons, piano lessons	☐ Babysitting, paper route

The number of checkmarks in each column will indicate whether you are the favored child or suffering as a victim of favoritism.

Unfortunately, there is little that can be done to alleviate the symptoms of this disease. Favoritism is incurable. There is only one known remedy: Be an only child.

A Classic Case of Favoritism

The ways in which we become petty, jealous, and envious as adults can be traced directly to the ways our mothers treated us in comparison to our siblings.

Take, for example, the case of Janey C., a successful public relations executive prone to jealous rampages and violent fits of envy.

"My mother always wanted to be a journalist, but she said she had to abandon her career because of her two kids, me and my brother, Jim," Janey explained during a recent interview. "But, even so, Mom's been writing poems for thirty years. She has boxes and boxes of them but she's never written one about me, her only daughter, and it really kind of bothers me.

"She's written tons of poems about my brother. *What Is a Son?* I could quote this poem verbatim from the time I was ten years old.

> What is he, do you suppose?
> Pockets bulging with rocks and toads
> Dreaming of fishing while in church
> Where will it end, this fugitive search?
> Doctor, lawyer, Indian chief—
> These thoughts bring me no grief—
> For no matter what he becomes,
> He will always be my son.

"Now, you should know that my brother did not turn out to be a doctor, lawyer, or Indian chief.

"He was always getting into trouble as a kid, and I mean serious trouble. Yet, my mother found all these wonderful things to say about him in her poems. She goes on writing poems about my brother and reciting *What Is a Son?*, the last time while we were on the bus going to Riker's Island, to *jail*, to visit my brother. He's doing time for passing bad checks and I don't know what else.

"My mother has written poems about our rowboat, her canary, even about her damned marinara sauce. Yet when I ask her to write about me, she says, 'I don't know what it is, Janey, but I just can't put pen to paper about you.' "

Is it any wonder then, that Janey moved 3,000 miles away from her mother and absolutely refuses to visit her brother in prison any more?

Sibling Solidarity

Occasionally, siblings can and do form an allegiance which psychologists call Sibling Solidarity. Usually, this happens when children share a mutual bond or have survived a trauma together. Say, for example, when the VCR went on the blink and there was nothing to watch for a whole evening, except reruns of *Three's Company*. Children can survive such catastrophes, and often, this kind of experience will draw siblings closer together for periods as long as twenty-four hours. In one such recorded case, two teenage sisters in Tacoma, Washington, remained civil to each other for an entire *weekend* after a thunderstorm brought down the family satellite dish and, for four days, disrupted all TV service (including HBO the weekend *Cocktail* premiered). Unfortunately, though, the kids' parents, Mildred and Frank Hosannah, had to be hospitalized for severe emotional trauma.

As the Hosannahs discovered, though it is difficult for parents to live with children who fight all the time, united siblings can pose an even greater problem. Once children discover that it is possible to transcend parental authority, all hell breaks out.

It is a simple law of family life that, as a unit, siblings can be more powerful than parents, especially if, together, children outnumber the adults in a given household.

Thus, Sibling Solidarity can also occur when children form a pact against their parents. This pact may involve sharing a secret such as:

- "We stayed up till midnight when Mom and Dad played bridge at the Conners."
- "We saw Mommy dent the Buick."
- "We lied to the babysitter."

- "We saw Daddy kissing Mrs. Conners."
- "We killed the cleaning lady and buried her in the basement."

Sibling Loyalty

Prolonged Sibling Solidarity can sometimes lead to Sibling Loyalty. Interesting, the word "loyalty" comes from the French word *loi*, which means law and does aptly apply when used to describe instances of sibling loyalty. That is, the first law among siblings, laid down by Mom: If you don't take care of your sister, Mom and Dad will kill you.

There are several distinct characteristics of sibling loyalty. See if any apply to you and your sister.

- Sisters are helpful and cooperative and do not strangle each other while Mom is in the bathroom.
- They resolve conflicts without spilling any blood or breaking any major bones.
- They occasionally compliment each other, unaccompanied by rude noises or obscene gestures.
- They help each other with homework or chores without expecting a million favors in return.
- They lend each other items of clothing without financial remuneration; they lend money without charging exorbitant interest.
- They do not auction off items of personal apparel, such as sister's brassiere, to the highest bidder among the neighborhood boys.
- They protect each other when attacked by outsiders, especially schoolmates criticizing a sibling's burgeoning sexuality.
- They do not air their differences in front of company, especially Daddy's boss or Mommy's old maid cousin Helen from Des Moines.

- They do not draw mustaches, beards, or black teeth on a sister's graduation picture.
- They do not use baby siblings as basketballs, hockey pucks, or first-base bags.
- They become upset if the other sibling is punished and will try to prevent sibling punishment by occasionally taking the blame when Mom's best Waterford crystal gets smashed.
- They make nice and give kisses to each other in front of witnesses.
- They do not lock each other out of the house or demand ransom for small favors.
- They do not abandon one another in the middle of a major crosswalk or at the mall.
- They do not hide in laundry hampers or broom closets for the sole purpose of scaring the other sister to death.
- They do not react to a sibling's new boyfriend by sticking their fingers down their throat and pretending to barf.
- They do not embarrass each other by revealing intimate family secrets to prospective friends and/or dating partners.

Sibling Contamination

During middle childhood, one of the most common problems among sisters is the fear of sibling contamination. One sibling, usually the oldest, worries that she will catch something from her younger sisters. She expresses her fear of sibling contamination by asserting that one or more of her sisters ". . . has got the cooties!"

For many decades, parents and psychologists have wondered: "What exactly are the cooties?"

Technically, cooties encompass a wide range of distinguishing attributes but are generally acknowledged as any character trait that is uncool or, in today's parlance, "not fresh." Cooties include—but are not limited to—the inability to dance, bad taste in clothes, any hairstyle that does not require $5.75 worth of mousse, and the penchant for acquiring stupid best friends. In short, cooties are a euphemism for any form of nerdy behavior.

The assumption that a sibling possesses cooties relates to an unconscious fear that a sister's major personality flaws may be hereditary. Thus, a prime question sisters ask is: "If my sister's a geek, am I doomed?"

This fear is so dominant that, at a remarkably early stage of development, sometimes even before language skills or potty training, children learn the techniques required for cootie prevention.

There is only one accepted method for cootie defense: the time honored practice of spraying the cootie victim with invisible cootie spray.

The technique involves holding up an invisible aerosol can and emitting a hissing sound by whistling through the teeth. At the same time, the technician may also exclaim: "Spraying for cooties!" (Younger children may not be sufficiently mature to include such declarations. In most cases, a simple "Pssst!" will suffice.)

The desired result of the cootie defense method is to humiliate the cootie-infested sibling and send her crying to Mommy. While cootie spraying has proven remarkably effective, recently many states have placed severe restrictions on the practice. In deference to our decaying ozone layer, cootie spraying has been banned in California, Florida, South Dakota, and Alaska. Pending legislation may obliterate the practice in several other parts of the country as well.

Concerned environmentalists promote a more practical solution to sibling contamination. Their organization is called STOP, signifying: "Save The Ozone, Please!" (We applaud the acronym for promoting a major environmental issue and being both grammatically correct and polite.)

STOP's primary agenda is to persuade siblings to "Stop Cootie Spraying! Start Separating!"

The STOP handbook advises: "If you fear cootie contamination, do not reach for the invisible aerosol can. Just say no, thank you. Separate yourself from infested siblings by staying in your room, locking the door, and wearing an industrial strength Walkman. Rubber gloves and surgical masks won't hurt either."

Recognizing that there are times when a child cannot escape the presence of her cootie-head sister, STOP offers an alternative plan. When siblings are forced to occupy the same space, STOP recommends they draw invisible boundary lines between themselves to prevent the spread of cooties. "Always carry an invisible piece of chalk in your pocket for such an emergency," advises STOP president, Merrill Barkow.

When confined to the back seat of the family car, for instance, siblings should carefully delineate their individual territories with an invisible line drawn down the middle of the vehicle. If a sibling's arm or leg happens to cross this boundary line, it is permissable to interrupt the family game of License Plates or State Capitals by hair-pulling or raucous screams of "Get your fat foot off my side."

A more permanent STOP defense tactic is for siblings to arm themselves with certifiable proof that they are completely different from their sibling. This is achieved by hanging out with different types of kids and participating in different activities. One child may claim a sport—such as track and field or wrestling—and devote all of his or her energies to excelling in that sport. Her sister may study hard and become The Brain in the family. Another sibling may take up acting. Another may eat everything in sight and become the child with the weight problem.

In the next section, we will explore the various roles children assume to avoid sibling contamination and to establish separate but distinct identities from each other.

Establishing Your Place in the Family

Almost from birth, you learn to assert your identity by assuming a particular personality. This is necessary in order to establish your separateness from your siblings, especially since your mother is always calling you by your sister's name.

So, you are either Miss Popularity or the Spoiled Brat, the reliable child or the Flake, the organized one or the Sick-o. These personality labels will stay with you long after you are grown and have children of your own.

Many studies have been done to define the different routes a child can take in her emotional development. According to sociologists F.G. Boll and K.R. Chain, there are basically eleven roles that children assume in order to establish their place in the family structure.

Which one are you? Which one is your sister?

1) Miss Responsibility

This sister is always left in charge of her siblings when Mom and Dad play poker at the Schneiders' on Saturday night. She is the child who will know what to do if a stranger knocks on the door (*Don't answer!*) or if brother Kevin stays up till midnight to watch dirty movies on the Playboy Channel. (Collect $5.00 from Kevin or tell Mommy in the morning.) Other siblings refer to her as "the narc."

Most times, but not always, Miss Responsibility is the first-born child. In later life, it often comes as a shock to her to learn there is not necessarily a reservation in heaven for those who always empty the dishwasher.

2) Miss Smarty Pants

This child excels in school. She works hard, gets good grades, and is promoted as a role model to her fellow siblings by her parents. She is often asked to assist with her sister's homework or with Dad's weekly sales report.

Also known as the "Teacher's Pet," Miss S. Pants never has the time or inclination to learn how to ice skate, roller skate, or join in any activity that involves a ball, a motor skill, or a teammate. She is rarely very popular. She is prone to write reams of unmetered poetry and see a lot of Saturday afternoon movie matinees. In later life, she will excel in computer science, medicine, or law. She will make a lot of money and often be hit up for loans from siblings and parents.

3) Miss Popularity

The phone never stops ringing for this sister. She uses her charm and good cheer to win friends and influence peers. She is popular everywhere, except among her sisters.

Miss Popularity will probably marry young and have children before anyone else in the family. She will think of herself as the lucky one in the family.

However, Miss Popularity does not realize, until it's too late, that her role in life becomes severely compromised by the advent of stretch marks. In later years, she will smoke Virginia Slims and have trouble with her gums. She will worship Joan Collins.

4) Miss Social Butterfly

As opposed to Miss Popularity, Miss Social Butterfly goes out a lot but is often not very well liked, a situation which only makes her work harder. She will join every club in school, run for every office, and collect stray animals, particularly hamsters and kittens.

Miss Social Butterfly does not form lasting relationships, although she doesn't understand why. She believes in astrology, poignant comic strips, and group therapy. In later life, she will frequent singles bars, vacation at Club Med, and participate weekly in the Lottery.

5) Miss Super-Organized

Often isolated from the rest of the family, the organized child is a real drag to have around during picture-taking time as she will insist that everyone stand in height order. Her credo in life is: "A place for everything and everything in its place." Scuff marks on her sneakers (or yours) will drive her crazy.

As an adult, the organized child succeeds famously in corporate life, usually at the expense of her social life. She will own a co-op, organize her spices in alphabetical order, and, in private, religiously read the Personals.

6) Miss Sick-O

She whines, she moans, she gets headaches. She is the first to catch "that awful flu going around" and the last to recover from it. Her period causes more cramps than Montezuma's Revenge. She is often bloated.

She will marry rich and divorce early. She will complain about alimony and PMS.

She will think it a compliment when people call her a Princess.

7) Miss Flake

Very early in life, Miss Flake realizes that if she leaves her clothes and toys on the floor, someone else will pick them up. After that, she is relatively useless to her siblings, except during the late adolescent years when she will be the best source for illicit drugs.

Miss Flake will experiment with sex at an early age and get very good at it. She will be attracted to men who ride motorcycles. She will marry often and have many children who will be surprisingly adept at taking care of her.

8) Miss Klutz

She trips, stumbles, and falls. She stubs her toe, knocks over the milk, drops the dishes. She is a walking disaster, her nails are constantly chipped. She goes through life with Band-Aids on her knees and Ace bandages around her ankles. She constantly apologizes for her clumsiness and then breaks your favorite knickknack.

She is too nervous to date so she develops a wide range of girlfriends. She dreams of becoming Miss America and practices walking with a book on her head.

In later life, she will have trouble learning how to drive and may develop agoraphobia. She will go to extraordinary lengths to make sure her children take ballet lessons and play the piano.

9) Miss Tomboy

A complete opposite to Miss Klutz, Miss Tomboy will excel in every major sport. She plays kickball with a vengeance, tennis like a pro, and basketball until she sweats. She prides herself on never having thrown a softball underhand in her whole life.

She plays catch with Dad and is the first one picked for any team. She will fall in love with her junior high school gym teacher and never wash her gym shorts.

In later life, she will wear comfortable shoes no matter what the occasion.

10) Miss Spoiled Brat

Usually the youngest, the Spoiled Brat is babied most of her life by the other members of the family. All of her needs are met, all of her desires fulfilled, if not by her parents then by her siblings. The Brat does not think of herself as spoiled; she believes she is only getting what she rightfully deserves from life.

As an adult, she will own an American Express Gold Card, very expensive underwear, and order Chinese takeout at least three times a week.

11) Miss Miscellaneous

This is the catch-all category for those sisters born at the bottom of the sibling heap. Pity poor Miss Miscellaneous!

Like most younger siblings from very large families, Miss Miscellaneous is confounded to discover that all the good stuff is taken.

Such was the case for Elizabeth W., the youngest of twelve children. Elizabeth's older siblings had staked out almost every possible category. Her sisters and brothers had already assumed generic positions as: The Brain, The Football Player, The Juvenile Delinquent, The Dancer, The Actress, The Basketball Star, The Nerd, The Beauty, The Skater, The Math Whiz, and The Nincompoop. Elizabeth, a desperate but remarkably resourceful Miss Miscellaneous, developed a fascination for taxidermy.

Other Miss Miscellaneous siblings have been known to excel in stamp collecting and nail wrapping.

TEEN SISTERS: THE LIPSTICK WARS

Remember that as a teenager you are at the
last stage in your life when you will be
happy to hear that the phone is for you.
                                    —Fran Lebowitz

Learning to Share and Other Contradictions

For a sibling of any age or economic status, nothing is more painful or difficult to grasp than the concept of sharing. "You must share everything," parents tell their children, "but you cannot play with Mommy's things."

At an early age, children accept the idea that they must share their stuff with classmates or kids in the neighborhood because, if they don't, they won't have any friends. Thus, sharing becomes the logical means to an important end. But the point of sharing anything with a sibling is difficult, if not impossible, for children to comprehend. A kid's sense of reason runs along these lines: My sister will always be my sister—no matter how badly I treat her, so why bother sacrificing anything? "Why should I be nice to *her?*" sisters want to know. "What's in it for me?"

The situation is complicated by the fact that sharing with a sibling is not only a matter of taking turns with the kickball or waiting in line at the water fountain, sibling sharing goes far behind these small acts of generosity.

Here is what parents require of sisters: You must share your playthings, your bedroom, your meals, your bath, your bedtime, your school, your teachers, your rewards, your punishments, your friends, your family, your tape deck, your dog, your computer, your life, liberty, and pursuit of happiness—*all without showing any signs of jealousy, resentment or envy!*

Here's what children wonder: Are my parents crazy, or what?

The answer is no, they're not crazy. From the very beginning, your parents actually intended to do the best job of parenting they possibly could—which only makes it all the more astounding how they managed to muck up everything.

The problem is that parents live under the basic misconception mentioned at the beginning of this book, namely that: "Sisters who love each other don't fight." Ha! As we have seen, sisters who love each other do nothing but fight, especially during childhood, adolescence, young adulthood, and old age.

Before you were born, your parents—especially Mom—harbored the illusion that you and your sister would be kind, loving, and/or generous with each other. In fact, Mom might tell you that she actually gave birth to a second child for the express purpose that, with two, you'd each have someone to share everything with. (This reasoning will remain totally senseless until you, too, reach your childbearing years.) Mom's desire was manifest in various maternal fantasies. When Mom discovered she was pregnant, she probably thought, "Won't it be great for our daughter to have a sweet little baby sister? They will share everything. They can be best friends, go to school together, date each other's male friends. Maybe we'll make a double wedding. And I'll have *two* daughters to take care of me in my old age!"

Daddy thought, "Well, they'll always have each other after we're gone." Or, "They'll play together like me and my brother Billy!"

Of course, all parents suffer from selective memory when they are expecting a new child. (You probably will, too!) Mom conveniently forgets the part where she and her sister fought like cats and dogs throughout their childhood and didn't speak to each other from May 1954 to January 1957.

Dad barely recalls all the times his older brother Billy socked him in the nose.

Let's face it, it's confusing to be a parent. You want your child to have everything but you don't want to spoil her. You want her to learn from your years of experience without having to go through the experience herself. You want her life to be perfect, even when you know that perfect lives don't even *exist!*

Because of such confusion, parents are often ambiguous and contradictory in the rules they lay down for their children. Despite the teachings of Dr. Spock and their own best of intentions, parents invariably choose to forget the past and their own life experiences and make everything up as they go along. (It's no coincidence that all parents eventually adapt the adage: "Do as I say, not as I do.")

The following are only a few of the hopelessly contradictory rules parents try to instill in their offspring.

Mom and Dad's Mixed Messages

1) Be completely loyal, but always rat on each other when we demand to know who's responsible for the mess.
2) Be very, very close, but totally different.
3) Be competitive, but never, never, never fight.
4) Help each other all the time with everything but learn to take care of yourself.
5) Be tolerant of your sister, but don't let her get away with anything while we're out of the house.
6) Cooperate with each other, but do everything our way.
7) Be aggressive, but don't hurt each other.
8) Enjoy playing together but never, ever tease, ridicule, taunt, or poke fun at each other. And no running in the house!

No wonder kids are often confused!

Of course, siblings adhere to their parents' set of mixed messages as best they can (not that they have a choice!). But, if sisters could write their own rules for each other, we would see an entirely different set of commands.

Sisters Rules for Each Other

1) Stay out of my closet.
2) Stay out of my hair.
3) Stay out of my room.
4) Stay out of my diary.
5) Stay out of my way.
6) Stay out of my makeup case.
7) Stay away from my friends.
8) Get off the phone.
9) Wait your turn.

The truth is: We share stuff because we have to, not because we want to, and because Mom wouldn't let us have anything at all if we didn't. But that doesn't mean we have to like it.

Despite what Mom says, this is not selfishness *per se*. It's human nature to be possessive. Why else does Mom have to own every piece of Depression glass ever displayed on a thrift shop shelf?

Some sisters are better at pretending to share than others, but for the majority, if any sibling had her way, she would get everything and her sister would be allowed bread and water and maybe one of the Raggedy Ann dolls without the button eyes. If sisters were free to express how they really feel, parents would hear this: "Give me all the attention and all the toys and send Rebecca to live with Grandma."

Sharing and Competing

The roots of selfishness can be traced back to the earliest stages of life. Almost from birth, you and your siblings are lumped together into one package. Instead of being "our baby daughter Patricia," you suddenly become one of "the girls," "the children," or "the kids."

This sets the stage of sibling competition. Upon this stage, almost anything can be the basis for a competitive match.

Siblings will argue over toys, clothes, who gets the biggest piece of candy, which TV show to watch, who gets to sit in the front seat, who gets to be the witch at Halloween, and who gets to be most in love with Bon Jovi, among many other things, events, people, and situations.

It is during the formative teen years that Mom and Dad try to impress upon you the importance of sharing. They direct an enormous amount of effort attempting to teach siblings how to get along. Several times a day they will remind you: "You must share and share alike."

Sisters are not allowed to get upset or angry over this dictum. "Don't make such a big deal," parents say. "Smile and you'll feel better." In what is known as the Smiling-Through-Clenched-Teeth School of Childrearing, arguments are instantly settled when Mom demands: "Now make up and tell her you love her. Right now, young lady!"

Obviously, in any of these disputes, the older sibling has the greater advantage. It is at this early stage of life that siblings learn one of the most basic, fundamental facts of life: Fights are almost always won by those who are bigger, stronger, and complain the loudest.

One of the major benefits of having a sibling is that we learn the basic skills of how to compete in today's society. Let's face it, we live in a competitive world. Every day, someone is out there working just a little bit harder than you, earning just a bit more money so that he or she can purchase a BMW 325i while you drive a Volkswagen Beetle.

So, too, youngsters learn at an early age that the one with the most Nintendos gets more friends to come over after school. A kid living in a room filled with a VCR, an Apple computer, and a 21-inch color TV gets to tell friends and siblings, "I'm somebody. Mom and Dad spent a fortune on me. What have you got to show for yourself?"

The urge to acquire more and be more popular than a sibling (or anyone in the neighborhood) can be traced to the games children play. When sisters fight over whose Barbie gets to wear the genuine mink stole, manage Barbie's Old

Fashioned Ice Cream Parlour, or drive the pink Corvette, they are mirroring the conflicts they will face later in life as grown women, in the boardroom or country club.

Comparing Sisters

Parents make sharing very difficult when they make comparisons between sisters. "Look at your sister's room," Mom will say. "Why can't you be neat and tidy like her?"

Or, "Your sister is so smart in school. Why can't you get the same grades as her?"

Or, "Why can't your hair curl like your sister's?"

Do mothers actually think such remarks will make siblings want to change their behavior? In truth, Mom's comparisons have the almost exact opposite effect. If one sister is neat and tidy, the other becomes even more sloppy and untidy. If one sister is smart, the other decides school isn't all that important and joins the local motorcycle/acid rock group. If one sister's hair curls nicely, the other bleaches her hair blonde and mousses it into razor-sharp spikes. In such a way do the differences between siblings become a kind of self-fulfilling prophecy. Thus, hopefully, teaching Mom to keep her comparisons to herself.

Psychiatrists will tell us that all of these efforts to be different from our siblings are our attempts at establishing separate identities. One of a child's earliest notions is that of "mine" and "yours," which is why toddlers develop a firm attachment to a security blanket or stuffed animal. Later, the blankie and teddy bear will be replaced by a fur coat and pure breed Akita but the principle remains the same.

How To Get Your Piece of the Action

There's an old saying: "The squeaky wheel gets the grease." And, this rule also applies in childhood. As most parents will reluctantly acknowledge, "The whiny child gets the ten-speed bike."

It's a simple law of family life that a parent can only withstand a finite amount of whining. Thus, children learn, early enough, that begging, pleading, and praying aloud—when combined with compliments such as "You are the BEST mommy in the whole world"—is a cost-effective means of material gain.

In a competitive environment, such as the dining room table at dinnertime, children often employ several attention-getting devices such as giggling, throwing food, and banging feet against their chairs. While these techniques are effective in getting a parent's attention, they may also backfire and get you dismissed from the table before dessert.

Children also discover the value of sacrificing a sibling for greater personal gain. Thus, children become adept at spotting and relating any sibling wrongdoing (known in most families as "tattletaling") for the sole purpose of self-promotion.

For example, little Sybil will feel compelled to tell Mom and Dad that sister Sarah was seen necking in the basement with Rocky Rissoto after school that afternoon. While Sybil may be risking the threat of sibling retribution, the thrill of watching her sister being punished may offset any such fear for the younger sibling. Also, Sybil knows that while Mom and Dad are yelling at Sarah, they are unlikely to inquire about the C— that Sybil received on her algebra test.

In a similar tactic, siblings will attempt to make their sisters look stupid in order to appear better by comparison. This is called boosting yourself at your sister's expense. By repeatedly telling a sister she is dumb, the more clever sibling can often make herself appear smarter than she really is. A C+ may not look so bad when compared with a sibling's D.

Manipulation is another tactic often employed for gaining a fair share of the parental pocketbook. "If you really loved me, you'd let me go to Europe with the French club," is a tried and true method used during adolescence. The odds are increased with the added reminder, "All of my friends are going." Of course, this addendum may cause parents to fall back on the tired adage: "If all your friends were going to jump off a bridge, I guess you would, too!"

Communication:
The Fine Art of Bickering

In the eternal struggle for fairness, equality, and a bigger piece of the parental pocketbook, siblings create their own methods of communication. We will discuss the traditional forms of sibling torture in the next section. Here, we want to turn our attention to verbal communication.

The language mode most commonly used between siblings is called bickering.

A careful blending of sarcasm, irony, and teasing, bickering has its own distinctive cadence and rhythm and is as difficult to master as French, Spanish, or any elective second language. Like Chinese, the fine points of bickering can be discerned in the subtle rise and fall of the voice. If not practiced properly, bickering can be mistaken for its less sophisticated counterpart: whining.

Siblings speak the language of bickering in order to defend their own turf, compete with each other, and express resentment without being obviously nasty and invoking the wrath of their parents.

Bickering is an important element in the parry and retreat tactics inherent in any sibling relationship. Metaphorically speaking, bickering is the hidden kick under the kitchen table, the sly pinch behind Mom's back, the subtle shove in the ribs—a swift but deadly accurate maneuver that leaves no visible damage discernible to the parental eye.

Like a great game of tennis or championship chess, bickering is a delicate interplay of point/counterpoint. One well-modulated insult breeds another, then another, and so on. Needling is subtly employed. Time out is called when either opponent sticks out her tongue or one player turns crybaby and retreats.

Bickering is such an elusive art form that no handbook

exists to teach parents its fundamental principles. But we can begin to discover the rudimentary elements of this form of communication in the following verbatim transcript, recorded by a hidden microphone for our scientific research in the finished basement of the Fudderman house in Rockville Centre, Long Island, New York.

We are listening to a typical conversation between the two adolescent Fudderman sisters. Tiffany is fourteen and a half; her sister, Heather, is thirteen. The girls attend junior high school and have been bickering almost constantly since Heather first started talking in 1978. Listen carefully for the subtle nuances:

HEATHER: So, like Tiffy goes, so I'm going to the mall and so she goes and so I go out and she's like *gone* so, like of course, when I go back in, like what am I supposed to do? I tell her friends that she's gone. (*Voice is emphatic, but not too defensive*)

TIFFANY: Yeah, right, like Heather you are such a liar. (*Accusation!*) She tells them I went to the mall and like they all left without me.

HEATHER: Well, excuse me for living! (*Sarcastic*) But you know you shouldn't say you're going when you're not. (*Needling!*)

TIFFANY: I *was* going (*Defensive*) but I was waiting outside for them to pick me up and Simon came by.

HEATHER: You go, "I'm going to the mall," and then you go so I'm supposed to know you haven't gone? Like what am I? A mind reader or something? (*Three rhetorical questions in a row—very effective point-making*)

TIFFANY: No, you're a spaz. (*Needle*)

HEATHER: Yeah? Well, it takes one to to know one. (*Counter needle*)

TIFFANY: Oh, that's *really* clever, Heather. Like she's just so cool. (*Not a compliment!*)

HEATHER: You shouldn't say you're going to the mall and then not do it. (*Good rebuttal, Heather!*)

TIFFANY: You're not listening to what I'm saying! (*Evasive tactic, Tiffy. Let's see if it works!*)

HEATHER: You shouldn't say "I'm going to the mall" and then go out and talk to Simon. (*Heather scores by resorting to previously effective rebuttal*)

TIFFANY: Well, I was going to the mall but I was only talking to Simon while I waited for them to pick me up. (*Tiffany uses repetition to stick to her main line of defense*)

HEATHER: Simon is her boyfriend. (*Teasing*)

TIFFANY: At least I have a boyfriend. (*Catty, but effectively makes Heather pause and consider her next move*)

HEATHER: You didn't stay at the mall very long. (*Heather is making nice*)

TIFFANY: I forgot my wallet. (*Pretty dumb*)

HEATHER: Did you buy anything? (*Equally dumb: Obviously the Fudderman parents are no geniuses*)

TIFFANY: How could I buy anything if I forgot my wallet? (*Rhetorical sarcasm*)

HEATHER: You shouldn't have forgotten it then. (*Rhetorical needling, a very sophisticated form of bickering*)

TIFFANY: Heather, you are so obnoxious! (*Watch out— Tiffany's temper is beginning to flare. Things may get interesting*)

HEATHER: You said you were going to the mall so I told them what you said. (*Heather is a stickler for detail*)

TIFFANY: I don't want to discuss this anymore because you are just repeating yourself. (*Tactic known as the I-am-taking-my-ball-and-going-home*)

HEATHER: Well, you shouldn't have mentioned it. (*Oh, can it Heather*)

TIFFANY: I shouldn't do this, I shouldn't do that.

HEATHER: Yeah, you shouldn't.

TIFFANY: It's all your fault.

HEATHER: It is not.

TIFFANY: You're not listening!

HEATHER: I am, too. (*Repetitive point/counterpoint tactic*)

TIFFANY: Are not.

HEATHER: Am, too. (*Grammar is going to pot, girls!*)

Note: Final four comments are repeated ad infinitum—or until seven-thirty, when *Wheel of Fortune* goes on the air.

Alternate Modes of Sibling Torture

Adolescence is a time in childhood development when siblings begin to express themselves through alternative means. As explained in the previous chapter, siblings speak to each other through the language of bickering. Soon they advance to more sophisticated means of expression.

For this reason, psychiatrists, parents, and especially sisters often call the advent of adolescence "The Reign of Terror" and with good cause. The teen years represent the era when sisters learn and refine various techniques for browbeating each other.

1) Fighting
This is always a favorite, especially among the older, stronger, and more powerful siblings. Methods include

kicking, biting, scratching, pinching, hair-pulling, slapping, punching, gouging, or any other means that recklessly disregards a sibling's well-being.

Children soon discover that the only central commandment when physically abusing a sibling is to not attack any area between the nose and the hairline. From an early age, they are reminded of the most sacred parental admonishment, "You could poke out an eye!" Since parents never say, "You could poke out an ear drum" or "You could poke out your sister's pituitary gland," children learn that any body part other than the eyeball is open for attack.

Most sibling fights end only with the arrival of a parent, guardian, babysitter, or law enforcement official. An adult will try to talk rationally to the fighting siblings, to break up the dispute, and to demonstrate to children that, among mature, thoughtful adults, arguments can be settled in a calm, peaceful manner. A child really learns a lot about adult behavior by hearing an older authority figure scream at the top of their lungs: "I don't care who started it—you both go to your rooms and get out of my sight. If I hear you fighting anymore I'm going to kick the crap out of both of you!"

Once the authority figure leaves, the siblings are then free to work out their differences using traditional means, as mentioned above—biting, kicking, scratching, hitting, and spitting.

Parents should not be too bothered if their children fight frequently. Fighting is an important means of getting attention. "Sibling conflict is the normal means of working out childhood aggression," reports Dr. Momsuch. "Sibling conflict has only gone too far when it involves attempted drownings, poisonings, and/or setting siblings on fire."

2) Verbal Abuse

Name-calling, taunting, curse words, and ferocious teasing are the main aspects of verbal abuse between siblings. Annoying as this method may seem, it has been noted that prolonged verbal abuse can help increase vocabulary, diction, and voice projection.

Teasing may take many forms. Siblings are particularly sensitive in areas of body development, skin blemishes, stupid haircuts, or physical handicaps such as poor vision, crooked teeth, etc. Any embarrassing moment or humiliating experience (especially with members of the opposite sex) is considered a prime target. Failures at school, in the playground, or, again, among members of the opposite sex are also prime areas for teasing.

3) The Copycat Method

A truly effective means of sibling torture is The Copycat Method. This involves repeating everything the sibling says over and over. This method is so effective that it generally provokes siblings to escalate their differences into full-fledged physical abuse. No one in their right mind can stand hearing their words repeated over and over.

Freud wrote extensively about this phenomenon in his 1932 paper entitled, "The Repetition Syndrome, The Repetition Syndrome, The Repetition Syndrome."

4) The Most Effective Torture Method

Granted: Physical abuse is terrible, no one likes to be teased, and everyone hates a copycat, but there is, by far, a much more effective means of torturing a sibling. When you get really, really mad and want to seriously torture a sibling: *Totally ignore her.*

Siblings are resilient and can take almost anything from their sisters and brothers *except* being ignored.

5) Combination Platter

Most siblings learn early enough to employ all four methods of sibling torture. Combined into the "Teasing-Ignoring" Cycle, this can really drive a sister or brother up the proverbial wall. This cycle involves four easy steps:

a) Relentlessly tease your sibling until she gets mad enough to strike.
b) Copy everything she says and does.
c) Either use your superior strength to bring the sibling to her knees or your speed to get out of her way.
d) Ignore her completely.

Teaching Your Sister About S-E-X

Sisters have always served as role models to their siblings for learning about sexuality and sexual behavior. We find documentation way back in ancient times, in such popular cultural phenomenona as the hit folk song, "I Wish I Could Shimmy Like My Sister Kate."

As has already been discussed in earlier chapters (were you paying attention?), siblings teach each other about jealousy and envy, which comes in very handy when they begin having relationships with members of the opposite sex.

Aside from jealousy and envy, though, many other aspects of human sexuality become known through sibling relationships.

How we dress, for example, is an important barometer of our sexuality and how we feel about ourselves. We can learn a lot about children by being sensitive to their habits and manners. When a sister asks to borrow her older sibling's cashmere sweater, for example, she is saying that she admires her sister and wants to look like her. When a sister takes a younger sibling's favorite suede shoes, without asking, and then carelessly ruins them by wearing them in the rain, she is saying, "I'm selfish, so what?" And when a younger brother asks to try on his sister's strapless prom dress, he is saying, in effect, "When I grow up, I want to be Diana Ross."

Sisters readily take cues from each other and model themselves on their sibling's behavior. They compare bodies and imitate each other's sexual activities.

Through countless incidents over the course of adolescence, an older sibling can have an enormous influence over a younger sibling. She may teach her sister how to put on lipstick, how to kiss, when to start dating, or "go steady." She can show her sister how to gracefully turn down a date, avoid a boy's advances, and when to say "Stop that or I'll kick you where it really hurts!"

Parents may be uncomfortable discussing sex with their children and are, therefore, relieved by the fact that sisters can talk to each other. Before parents feel too secure, however, they should realize that older sisters can, and probably will, also teach their younger siblings about French kissing, smoking, hickies, drive-ins, making out, stealing money, taking Dad's car without permission, smoking pot, and experimenting with various illegal substances.

Thus, sisters can also have a negative influence on their younger counterparts. Inexperienced younger siblings may be confused by the advice given them by their older sisters and will simply follow everything they are told. How do they know when their sister is no longer a "proper" role model? As the noted psychologist Dr. Momsuch has advised her young patients: "If you suspect your older sister has turned into the town tramp, then for heaven's sake, don't borrow her underwear."

Playing Old Maid—for Keeps

It is not unusual in families with more than one daughter for one of the sisters to suffer from a psychological disorder called narcissism. This state of mind derives its name from the ancient myth of Narcissus, a beautiful young Greek youth who was transfixed by his own reflection in a pool of water. Unable to pull himself away from his own image, Narcissus eventually died of sorrow because he was denied the one thing he most adored: himself.

This story has long been the basis for clinical analysis of extreme individual self-absorption and may well apply to your very own sister. The modern equivalent of Narcissus is the teenager who sits in front of her dressing table all day and stares at herself in her vanity mirror. She is preoccupied with alternately tweezing and bleaching every hair above her neckline. Her twin heroes are Max Factor and Charles Revlon. She owns forty-seven different shades of lipstick but will not lend one of them to her sister.

The narcissistic sister will take a lion's share of the family's compliments and clothes budget. She will insist on having her own phone, and nothing less than a pink Princess phone will do.

A great example of the narcissistic sister was the character Ada, Joan Crawford's older daughter in the Oscar-winning movie *Mildred Pierce*. Ada got all the pretty new dresses and piano lessons, her younger sister got pneumonia and died in the first thirty minutes of the movie. Typical.

It's no wonder, then, that sisters of narcissists develop their own emotional traumas. Unable to compete in the beauty department, these hapless sisters are usually forced to rely on their personalities to win friends and attract boys. They learn how to carry on a decent conversation, the art of listening, and the importance of a sense of humor. Such attributes enable them to succeed brilliantly in later life, but no matter how rich and famous they eventually become, they never feel they are as attractive or popular as their narcissistic sisters. In short, they'd give up everything if they could just shimmy like their sister Kate.

Table: Major Patterns in the Relationship Between Teen Sibs

Modes of Behavior	Table of Behavior
Authoritative	"It's your turn to set the table."
Non-negotiable	"I set it yesterday."
Threatening	"I'll tell if you don't get those dishes right now!"
Helpful	"You forgot the napkins."
Fawning	"You set so much better than me."
Hostile	"The forks go on the left, idiot."
Really, Really Hostile	"You never set. I hate you."
Mutually Dependent	"I'll set if you clear."
Whining	"I always do the dishes."
Compromising	"Let's order in pizza."

ADULT SISTERS: THE SALAD BAR DAYS

You can tell your sister to go to hell in ten different languages, but if you need a dime she'll give you one.
—Elizabeth Mead Steig,
sister of Margaret Mead

Wedding Bell Blues:
When One Sister Marries
And the Other STAYS
SINGLE

Question for single gals . . . Tell the truth, which do you prefer: attending a wedding without a date or undergoing root canal without anesthesia? Close choice, huh? And why shouldn't it be? Even under the best of circumstances, weddings are nothing more than a $20,000 reminder that all the good guys are taken.

As any single woman will tell you, the only thing worse than attending a wedding is attending a *family* wedding. Then you have to contend with relatives who wink knowingly and ask in a booming voice: "So, when will I dance at your wedding?" They will ask the same thing of your date or the interesting guy you just met. "Wouldn't she make a beautiful bride?" your Auntie Miriam will ask the waiter standing nearby.

But, by far, the very worst single gal nightmare is attending her sister's wedding, especially if she is a younger sibling.

Finding Mr. Right or Mr. Good Enough

Even under normal circumstance, the two most dreaded words in a single woman's vocabulary are *"and Escort."* When attending your sister's wedding, the idea of getting a date is even more imperative. Remember: Her wedding pictures will become part of your family heritage for the rest of your natural life, so you must either find a photogenic guy or suffer decades of making excuses to every stupid cousin who looks at your sister's wedding album.

Naturally, the wedding is planned several months (sometimes years) in advance so you have plenty of time to ponder: Should I invite the guy I've been dating recently? Will I still be seeing him by the time the wedding arrives? If I ask him to be my escort will he suddenly develop a terminal case of car trouble?

Past experience has taught single women that attending weddings in general, and a close family wedding in particular, is not the best catalyst for a budding relationship. Often, the very idea of such an event triggers the I'm-Not-Yet-Ready-for-Any-Kind-of-Commitment automatic response programmed into any late model eighties man (even the new nineties man is prone to head for the hills at the thought of encountering entire generations of your family). So you must decide: Which is more important? A continuing relationship with that new guy or having a date for your sister's wedding?

The problem becomes more complex, of course, if you don't *have* a current guy. Then you'll spend hours with your Filofax, looking up old phone numbers to find an ex-boyfriend you might ask to the wedding. Scouting past relationships can be a very frustrating experience; you come to wonder why every guy you ever dated got married three months after he broke off with you.

So you consider asking your best male friend. This is your most secure move, but it's not without drawbacks: For a favor of this magnitude, even the best male friend demands a lot in return—like a complete home-cooked meal, followed by two videos of his choice. (Get ready for an Eastwood/Bronson double feature.) If you're lucky, your best friend will be nice and agree to a simple cash settlement.

Most importantly, no matter how much you hate the idea of attending yet another wedding, you don't want to give up the fantasy that your very own Mr. Right will be waiting to meet you at this particular affair. He'll be a friend of the groom, just in from assignment overseas. He'll look like Tom Selleck and move like Fred Astaire. Your eyes will meet across a crowded buffet table. He'll smile—and then notice your "date" tugging at your sleeve, begging to leave early. Mr. Right moves on. Is it worth the risk?

Perhaps it would be better to go it alone, you decide in a flash of Katharine Hepburn independence.

The High Cost of Your Reign as Maid of Honor

Almost as tricky as finding an escort is scaring up the money to pay for your sister's wedding present and the surprise shower you will be expected to throw. You don't

want to be chintzy because you really do love your sister, but truthfully, you'd rather spend the money on a new ski jacket.

Even after all the hard work and preparations, the hardest part of the shower is smiling your way through the grueling event. Surely, a sister's wedding shower is one of the most trying experiences in a single's woman's life. It's not so much that the talk centers around wedding dresses, bridesmaids, and honeymoons, or that the majority of the other women are all married. It's watching your sister open all those gifts and the strain of pretending not to be insanely jealous.

What really galls about being single is that no one ever thinks to buy you cheese trays with matching knives, candlestick holders, expensive sheets, silver frames, more than four of any type glassware, top-of-the-line toaster ovens or vacuum cleaners, ice buckets, serving platters, crystal vases, big salad bowls with matching individual bowls, matching dinnerware, matching place mats, matching napkins, matching anything, nice towels, washcloths, or anything monogrammed.

Not that you're bitter or jealous or anything, but when the wedding day arrives, you can't help feeling just a little bit elated if the weather is overcast, hazy, or raining cats and dogs (except, of course, if you've bought suede shoes to wear that day).

The Reception

As maid of honor, you will have the opportunity to walk down the aisle before your sister. All those people staring at you as you slowly march in time to the music . . . You know that every one of them is wondering why it isn't you in a white dress and veil (or is this just your imagination?).

During the actual ceremony, you are your sister's sidekick and your chores involve holding her bouquet, helping move her veil, or fixing the train of her dress. You will not need to work hard at these tasks, the hard part of your job at this stage of the wedding is convincing everyone your tears are from *happiness* for your sister.

During the reception, you will either be sitting at the main table with your sister or at a family table with your cousins. At some point, you'll want to make your way over to the "single table" to check out any likely prospects. No need to ask where this table is located—just head in the direction of the kitchen.

Here you will find the assorted reception riffraff—oddball cousins that no one really knows (or likes), an office acquaintance from Dad's old business firm, the lone next-door neighbor, or the lady who cleans house for the groom's parents. There may well be several single men at this table though, of course, they will be wearing brown shoes with their blue suits and none of them will know how to dance.

Inevitably, the dreaded moment arrives when the orchestra strikes up the first tune and everyone gets up to dance. You rush to the ladies room to freshen your lipstick. This works well for the first eight or nine tunes, but after a while, you begin to doubt that your lips are worth all this exercising and you head for the open bar instead.

The food, when it finally arrives, will be either cold, or fattening, or both. However, by this time you are either starving or too drunk to care, or both. So, in between trying to chit chat with your dinner companions, you eat everything put in front of you—and take seconds if they're offered. (You will suffer guiltily from these excesses in the morning.)

Sometime before dessert, the photographer arrives for the traditional "table photo." This causes yet another great dilemma: Should you disappear or pretend to be coupled with the guy standing next to you, even if he is your cousin Melvin from South Jersey?

More disturbing than the photographer, though, is the advent of the video cameraman who insists on not only recording your image (we know those videos add ten pounds to our hips) but wants to trap you into saying something on tape. You decline to speak on camera, he insists—all the while recording your desperate attempt to flee. To get away, you accept an invitation to dance from the guy in the three-piece, green plaid suit. But, just when you get to the dance

floor, there's that cameraman again, recording your efforts to keep in step with your partner's version of the Mashed Potato.

"You're Next!"

At your sister's wedding, there's no escaping the traditional tossing of the bridal bouquet. You know it's your mother's arm that shoves you toward the front of the group of squealing women. You dread getting involved in such an immature, ridiculous ritual—although, if you happen to catch the bouquet, you can't help thinking that maybe you will be the next one to marry. . . .

Sound Advice

Here are some tips for surviving your sister's wedding:

1) Don't go.
2) Go for the ceremony, get a headache, and leave before the reception.
3) If you must go, drink heavily. Flirt with the groom, ask him to dance, and slip him your phone number. With the divorce rate today, he may be available again

DURING THE FOLLOWING WEEKS, DENNIS WAS AT THE HOUSE OFTEN... AND ONCE...

LET'S GO FOR A DRIVE NOW, IRENE! THERE'S A VERY SPECIAL WATERFALL I WANT TO SHOW YOU THAT'S BEAUTIFUL IN THE MOONLIGHT.'

FIRST I HAVE TO HELP ADELE WITH THE DISHES.' THEN SHE CAN COME WITH US.'

I'LL DO NO SUCH THING.' HASN'T IT OCCURRED TO YOU THAT DENNIS MIGHT WANT TO BE ALONE WITH YOU ?

sooner than anyone suspects. And we all know how hard it is to find the marrying kind of man. Who knows? In a year or two, your sister may be worrying about getting a date for your wedding.

Timetable of Sisterly Love: The Gabors

1920s (possibly earlier)—Magda, Zsa Zsa, and Eva are born to Jolie and Vilmos Gabor in Hungary. Exact years of birth are never confirmed; in fact, as the decades progress the Gabors will claim they were born in the 1930s, meaning they married, for the first time, at about age nine.

1930s—As soon as legally possible, all three sisters are married: Magda to an impoverished Hungarian aristocrat, Zsa Zsa to a Turkish diplomat, and Eva to a still-in-training Swedish osteopath. All three marriages combust in spontaneous divorces.

1939—Eva moves to Hollywood to seek a career in the movies and marries Charles Isaacs, millionaire.

1942—Zsa Zsa follows Eva to Hollywood, also to pursue a film career, and marries Conrad Hilton, hotel baron and multimillionaire.

1940s—Zsa Zsa becomes addicted to uppers and Eva has her committed. Upset, Zsa Zsa tells the press Eva was jealous and reveals that her sister is living in sin with John Perona, owner of Club Morocco.

—Magda, in Budapest, has an affair with Dr. Carlos di Sampayo Garrido, a Portuguese ambassador who helps her, Mama Jolie, and Dad escape war-torn Hungary.

—Magda's arrival in New York is shrouded in mystery. Reporters wait for her dockside but she never appears. According to rumor, Eva and Zsa Zsa have Magda secretly smuggled out of her cabin and rushed by ambulance to a Long Island clinic for an immediate nose job. With a nose compatible to her sisters, Magda is presented to the New York press and, shortly thereafter, marries William Rankin, a Hollywood writer.

1946—Zsa Zsa divorces Hilton.

1949—Zsa Zsa marries character actor George (*All About Eve*) Sanders but they establish separate residences.

1951—Zsa Zsa's career soars after she appears as a panelist on an early TV talk show. She is offered ten movie

roles, twenty-five more TV appearances, and national publicity—thus achieving in a half hour what sister Eva had been unable to do in twelve years.

—Though still married to Sanders, Zsa Zsa begins a well-publicized affair with Porfirio Rubirosa of the Dominican Republic, recently divorced from tobacco heiress Doris Duke. During their three-year affair, Porfirio will wed another heiress, Barbara Hutton; their marriage will last seventy-three days.

1953—All three sisters appear together for the first time at the Frontier Hotel in Las Vegas. The show is called "The Gabor Sisters—This Is Our Life." The fact that none of them can sing or dance does not hinder their popularity.

—Mama Jolie insists on joining the act, too.

—Eva warns that she doesn't want to be lumped together with her sisters. "We are not the McGuire sisters," she informs the hotel manager.

—Opening night is disrupted when Zsa Zsa arrives with a black eye, courtesy of Porfirio. Mama Jolie, Eva, and Magda are furious about the subsequent embarrassing publicity.

1954—Zsa Zsa divorces Sanders. "Married life with Zsa Zsa was one of the great humiliations of my life," he later tells reporters.

1955—Magda attempts suicide with an overdose of sleeping pills after being dumped by boyfriend, Tony Gallucci.

1956—In April, Eva marries Dr. John Williams, a plastic surgeon.
   —In October, Eva divorces Dr. John Williams, has an affair with actor Tyrone Power, and marries Richard Brown.
   —Magda marries Tony Gallucci.

1960s—An accomplished actress in her own right, Eva is constantly mistaken for Zsa Zsa by fans. Joyce Haber, a *Los Angeles Times* columnist, later writes that ". . . survival in Hollywood means being able to tell one Gabor from the other."

1960s–1980s—Zsa Zsa marries and divorces: Joshua Cosden, oil baron; Herbert Hunter, chairman of Struther Wells Corporation; Jack Ryan, inventor (Barbie doll); and Mike O'Hara, lawyer.
   Many years later, Zsa Zsa would insist she *never* married for money and that she proposed to every one of her seven husbands (not all of them said yes the first time.)

1967—Magda's husband Tony Gallucci, dies and she suffers a stroke. Nursed slowly back to health, she fights for and wins a substantial portion of Gallucci's estate and becomes the richest Gabor sister.

1967–1972—Eva finally achieves recognition, fame, and wealth from her starring role in the popular TV series *Green Acres*. Her husband, Richard Brown, is made senior v.p. of the show.

According to Peter Brown, author of *Such Devoted Sisters: Those Fabulous Gabors*:

> One of the few things that drew her [Eva's] ire was *any* mention of Zsa Zsa. Fellow actors [on *Green Acres*] learned quickly that her sister was not a topic of conversation. Once when an actor quoted Zsa Zsa's witticism from a talk show, Eva snapped, "I don't quote President Johnson to you so why do you quote Zsa Zsa to me?"
>
> On the other hand, no one was allowed to criticize her sister. One afternoon, after seeing a somewhat bloated and disheveled Zsa Zsa on a late night talk show, another actor laughingly commented to Eva, "You know Miss Gabor, Zsa Zsa in a certain bad light looks more like villain Jack Palance."
>
> Her face flushed and her eyes narrowed. "Don't you *ever* criticize my sister again—ever!"

1969—Eva divorces Richard Brown after setting a Gabor record for the longest running marriage (thirteen years).

1970—Magda marries actor George Sanders (yes, Zsa Zsa's ex). They divorce six weeks later, setting the Gabor record

for the shortest marriage. Later, Sanders would say that dealing with the three sisters was "like confronting the Spanish Armada in a rowboat." He commits suicide at age sixty-five.

1973—Eva marries Frank Gard Jameson.

1976—Zsa Zsa and Eva appear together on the Chicago stage as the murderous sisters in *Arsenic and Old Lace.*

1983—Eva divorces Jameson.

Today—Magda, Zsa Zsa, Eva, and Mama Jolie make their home base in Palm Springs. Although they don't live together, each daughter calls her mother once a day.

—Zsa Zsa convicted of three misdemeanor charges on September 29, 1989 as a result of a confrontation with a police officer who stopped her car in June. The trial (and Zsa Zsa's wardrobe) make national headlines.

—Jolie tells a reporter, "In America, my girls were wealthy, famous, and unhappy. They were most dissatisfied with their men and with each other."

Why Your Sister's Grass Is Always Greener, and Her Carpet Always Cleaner

As adults, we know very little about how our sisters actually function in the real world. We tend to exaggerate and amplify. Somehow our sister's life seems better than our own. Also, we get stuck on images from childhood. Thus, if we thought our adolescent sister was the most popular girl in seventh grade, we tend to keep this image well into adulthood, even if Sis hasn't had a date since disco music and Donna Summers was Number One on the charts.

As teenagers, sisters have unreal fantasies about each other, but once sisters grow up and pursue different lifestyles, these misconceptions can become monumental. This is especially true if one sister is married and the other is single. Single women have unrealistic expectations of married life. Conversely, once a woman marries, she often forgets the hardships of single life. Thus, sisters of differing marital status have trouble realistically evaluating each other's daily life.

To illustrate this point, we asked the McKinsey sisters from New Point, Massachusetts, to tell us—in intimate detail—how they each imagined a typical weekend in their respective sister's life. We present both fantasies and then the opportunity for each woman to comment on how close her sister's fantasy fits reality. The results of this experiment may shock and disarm you, but not half as much as they shocked and disarmed the McKinsey sisters.

A Single Woman's Fantasy of Her Married Sister's Weekend

My married sister has this great job, she's the hostess for a local television show which I think she relishes because all her clothes are tax deductible. Anyway, she's married to the perfect man—a doctor, no less—who looks like a cross between Kevin Costner, Sean Connery, and Alex Manero. (*Note:* Alex is the guy I loved madly in seventh and eighth grades. I almost died when he moved away. Really. Almost died.)

My brother-in-law's a fantastic slow dancer and he thinks my sister's cellulite is "kind of cute." In fact, he recently insisted that she quit her aerobics class, saying, "You're

getting too thin. You should never exercise again in your whole life." Can you imagine?

I don't want to use real names, so call him Rhett. Call her Lucky.

This is sort of how I envision a typical weekend at their house—a lovely split-level in the suburbs of Chicago.

FRIDAY AFTERNOON: Lucky is able to leave work early, mainly because her two super-efficient, totally devoted assistants offer to work until midnight.

She drives home (no traffic, I'll bet), anxious to see her three adorable children, Joshua (ten), Jared (six) and Jennifer (two), and her live-in maid, Conceptia (twenty-five). The kids look like models and act like angels. None of them has ever uttered, "give me . . ." "take me . . ." or "buy me . . ." Conceptia speaks perfect English and does windows.

When Lucky arrives at the house, Jennifer is just awakening from her nap and the boys are returning from their school for gifted children. Lucky asks, "What did you learn in school today?" and Jared explains the basic principles of the multiplication table; Joshua answers in Japanese.

Everybody changes clothes and spends quality playtime together while the maid prepares dinner (did I mention that Conceptia is a gourmet cook?).

Rhett returns home from the hospital in time to play ball

with Joshua, build a model airplane with Jared, teach the alphabet to the baby, and massage Lucky's feet.

Because she looks tired, Rhett insists Lucky take a hot bubble bath while he helps feed, bathe, and get the kids ready for bed. Refreshed from her bath, Lucky offers to read a bedtime story and the boys select a thin book with only two sentences per page. By page 4, the children are fast asleep.

Then Rhett and Lucky share a candlelight champagne dinner. They dance to the soundtrack from *The Big Chill*. He gives her a dozen white roses because today is the twelfth anniversary of the day they met. Lucky reminds him that next week is the anniversary of their first kiss. He promises to buy her a new car.

He waltzes her upstairs to the master bedroom where they make love three times and fall asleep locked in each other's arms.

Conceptia does the dinner dishes.

SATURDAY MORNING: The children sleep until ten o'clock, as usual, and play quietly with each other until Mom and Dad wake up.

After breakfast, the family piles into the station wagon for a drive in the country. On the way, they pass a garage sale in progress, and knowing how much Mom loves a bargain, everyone eagerly agrees to stop. Lucky finds a complete and

THE REAL TRUTH ESCAPED MY LIPS...

BUT I'M SCARED.' SUPPOSING NOBODY ELSE EVER ASKS ME TO MARRY HIM.' YOU KNOW HOW FEW BOYS I'VE KNOWN... HOW FEW DATES I'VE HAD.'

OH, HONEY, DIDN'T I HAVE TO WAIT A LONG TIME? AND NOW I'M SO THANKFUL I DID.'

YOU'VE GOT TO MAKE UP YOUR MIND.' WILL YOU MARRY A MAN YOU DON'T LOVE --AND RISK A LIFE-TIME OF UNHAPPINESS? OR WILL YOU WAIT, AND HOPE TO FIND THE RIGHT MAN SOME DAY.' I HAD TO CHOOSE... SO MUST YOU.'

original twenty-four–piece set of Fiestaware, in assorted colors and perfect condition, for $35. She bargains with the owner and gets the price down to $15.

That night, Lucky decides to cook her favorite stir-fry dish so Rhett volunteers to go shopping at the local market and then washes, slices, and dices seven different vegetables.

After the kids are asleep, Rhett joins Lucky for a long talk in front of a roaring fire. He listens attentively to all her problems and calms her fears and anxieties, especially those left over from her single life. He vows to love her well into the next century and, in the year 2000, to be her date for New Year's Eve.

SUNDAY: Rhett insists on cooking breakfast for the kids and serving Lucky breakfast in bed. The whole family climbs aboard the king-sized, down-quilted, four-poster bed to eat with Mom. No one spills anything or gets crumbs in the sheets.

Joshua discusses a personal problem, listens attentively to his parent's opinions, thanks them for their advice.

At noon, the children are picked up by their grandparents so that Lucky and Rhett can spend the day together by themselves. They drive into the city, to their favorite little sidewalk café where they sit all afternoon—holding hands, whispering in each other's ear, giggling like two teenagers in love—and watch all the people on the street. Lucky counts

all the miserable single people who walk by and stare at her and Rhett enviously. By the time she reaches 487, she's ready to return home.

That night, the kids insist on catching the PBS Masterpiece Theater adaption of *Silas Marner*. No one touches the remote control.

During a boring pledge break, the *Chicago Sun Times* calls to inform Lucky she's been nominated for an Emmy, the Mrs. America Award, and the Nobel Peace Prize.

Lucky sighs contentedly. This weekend was almost as good as the one when she won the Illinois State Lottery.

A Married Sister Replies

First of all, for the record, children look like models and act like angels only when they're asleep. And husbands never make love more than once a night. Who gave my sister these ideas? And when can I meet him?

It's true that a mate will chop the veggies for stir-fry, although he refuses to do the dishes. He will hug you before you go to sleep, especially if he doesn't want to have sex that night.

But a husband will also tell you that you're not fat (at least mine will, and my sister can't have him) when you think you're so fat you deserve to die.

I should add, though, that live-in maids can either cook or speak English but never both. Nobody can even look at Fiestaware for under $200. And, I'm flattered, but I never won the Nobel Peace Prize, an Emmy, or the Lottery—although I once found a five-dollar bill in the bottom of a shopping cart.

Honestly, if my life ran as smoothly as my sister thinks, I wouldn't be living on Valium and twelve cups of coffee a day.

A Married Woman's Fantasy of Her Single Sister's Weekend

My sister doesn't know that she's the kind of woman everyone envies—tall, nice legs, . quirky sense of style. She has her Master's Degree in American Studies from Cornell and a honey-colored mink coat that matches her hair. She writes a weekly column for a major magazine and is working on a novel. She travels all over the country. I'll bet she's got a guy in every major city, and some suburbs as well. She's thirty-two, looks twenty-six, and is too happy to even think about settling down. Call her Scarlett.

FRIDAY EVENING: Scarlett takes a ballet class after work. Dancing is her hobby; she actually enjoys exercising. Can you imagine? After class, she attends a concert at Lincoln Center. She could've invited one of her many friends—the tickets are one of the perks of her job at the magazine—but after a week of city hubbub, appointments crosstown, and deadlines, she glories in being alone, a privilege her married-with-kids friends experience only in the bathroom (and sometimes not even then).

Walking home, Scarlett hums Mozart and thinks about her long-distance lover, Brian, a much acclaimed architect and mountain climber whose work and hobby take him around the world. Tomorrow he will interrupt an important weekend conference to spend twenty-four hours with her in New York. They haven't been together in weeks and won't see each other again for at least a month when they'll spend five days together in San Francisco. Scarlett loves this arrangement: She's attached but not obligated.

SATURDAY: After sleeping soundly until 11:00 A.M., Scarlett takes another dance class (she's as compulsive about dancing as she is about writing) and then has a massage and sauna at her health club. Her time and money are her own so she also gets her hair hennaed, her nails done, and a pedicure. Afterward, she shops in the gourmet food stores around Tribeca and buys champagne, figs, smoked salmon, and a baguette of French bread.

Scarlett passes a new clothing store and can't resist buying the little black dress featured in the window because everything in the shop is on sale. Then, in a shoe store near her home, she finds a pair of heels that perfectly match the dress, which she has to buy, even though the shoes cost three times the price of the sale dress.

Exhausted, Scarlett drops all her shopping bags on the island kitchen counter in the waterfront loft she bought several years ago. Her decorating style is soothingly minimalist: uncluttered, with only a few choice pieces of furniture, expensive Italian light fixtures, no toys. The space is dominated by a huge, built-in platform bed where she sleeps on silk sheets and satin pillows.

She puts Frank Sinatra and Ella Fitzgerald on the CD and adds imported bath salts to the running water in her sunken tub. Sipping wine from a crystal goblet, she luxuriates in the hot bath and daydreams about both Brian and an idea for next week's column. She anoints herself with creams and perfume after the bath and then applies her make-up at a marble dressing table in the bathroom.

When the bell rings, she answers the door barefoot, dressed only in the black lace lingerie Brian bought her in Paris. "Hello, love," he says as he rushes to embrace her.

Over dinner, he asks if she will spend the Christmas holidays with him in Greece. "Maybe," she demurs. "Perhaps I can be persuaded if you rent a villa overlooking the sea."

SUNDAY: Brian leaves about 3:00 P.M. and Scarlett sits

among the sexy disarray of her bed and thinks about him while she writes in her diary and scribbles notes for her novel. Then she telephones her best friend, Lena, and they decide to see a Woody Allen movie. Afterward, they head for their favorite neighborhood bistro.

The two friends eat seafood salad and cheesecake and discuss their respective Saturday night dates. They make plans to throw a big party next month when they'll invite all their old beaus.

As they talk, they're being watched by two men who are drinking beer and laughing in a corner booth. Scarlett looks up and recognizes one of the men as a fairly well-known painter; last week she attended the opening of his latest exhibit. He's tall and broad, with dark eyes and a reddish beard; his teeth are very white. He walks over to her table.

"Hello," he says, revealing an intriguing accent. "My name is Anton Orloff."

"I know," Scarlett grins.

He returns the smile. "I am very happy to meet you at this longing last."

"I'm very happy to meet you, too," Scarlett answers. And she is. At this longing last.

A Single Sister Replies

My sister got everything exactly right—except that I take jazz class, not ballet, the highlights in my hair tend more toward burnt sienna than honey, and I refuse to wear mink.[1]

Not to be picky, but my sister did fail to include a few minor details that will shed light about the realities of single life:

1) Brian is married.
2) The trip to Greece gets canceled when his wife finds our airplane tickets and threatens to commit suicide.
3) The payments on my waterfront loft are so high that I have to write three extra freelance articles a month just to cover the maintenance.

[1] I wear raccoon.

4) Usually, I don't get to sleep late on Saturday morning because that's when Mom calls to ask when I'm going to stop wasting my life, settle down, marry a doctor, and have three children like my sister.
5) Anton Orloff turns out to be gay.

Sister Scorecard: Jackie vs. Joan Collins

In the March 1988 issue of *Vanity Fair*, author Dominick Dunne interviewed both Joan and Jackie Collins for an in-depth analysis of the relationship between the two famous sisters. Ground rules for this article were established by Jeffrey Lane, who acted as publicist for both women. "If Jackie's name was used in one sentence, then Joan's name must be first in the next," wrote Dunne, "and there was to be equal copy on both sisters."

Did the article play by the rules? Did one sister outscore the other? Were there any penalties for foul shots?

Let's check the final scorecard:

	Jackie	Joan
Number of times name mentioned in article (including captions)	51	58
Sensitive subjects will not discuss with press	"Miss Collins will not discuss her sister."	None
First meeting with author Dunne	At Swifty Lazar's Oscar party at Spago	On beach in 1957

Quote about sister	"We're not the kind of sisters who call each other every day but she knows I'm there for her."	"I don't have a rivalry with my sister."

Personal History:

Age	Younger than Joan	56
Marriages	2	4
Divorces	0	4, ("I left all my husbands!")
Widowed	1	0
Children	Tracy, Tiffany, Rory	Tara, Sacha, Katyana
Last known affair	None	Bill Wiggins, known in British tabloids as Bungalow, "He has nothing upstairs and everything down below."
Home in L.A.	Formerly owned by Carroll Baker	Built by Laurence Harvey
Books published	11	2
Copies sold	65 million in 30 languages	A lot less
Parts in prime-time television	"The fact that I've been offered the lead in soap opera has nothing to do with [Joan writing a] book."	Alexis in *Dynasty*

| Lifestyle | Homebody, great housekeeper | Loves nightlife, great hostess |
| Official title in the Kingdom of Glitz | Queen of Dish | Queen of Soap |

Grown-Up Battles

Parents often think that sibling arguments are a function of childhood. "They'll grow out of it," parents think. "When they grow up they'll stop fighting and be nice to each other." Nothing could be further from the truth.

Adult sisters fight just as much—maybe more—than they did as adolescents or children. As adults, sisters have the advantage of maturity and wisdom, and thus, their fighting can be even more vindictive. By the time they reach adulthood, sisters have a great warehouse of old grudges and petty grievances against each other that they can summon at a moment's notice. A grown-up discussion over who should make Thanksgiving dinner can quickly escalate into a full-fledged fight about the time one sister accidentally scratched her sibling's favorite 45s. They say elephants never forget. Neither do sisters.

As evidence of how grown-up battles can be as bad—if not worse—than childhood battles, we present the true life story of two famous sisters who were notorious for airing their differences in public. The following factual case history is not only a great example of adult sisters squabbling but verifiable proof that I actually did research for this book.

Olivia De Havilland and Joan Fontaine

Well-known actresses, and sisters, Olivia de Havilland and Joan Fontaine were born in Tokyo. Olivia was a year older than Joan. Their parents divorced shortly after Joan was born and the girls moved to the U.S. with their mother. The sisters were always competitive and never got along as children. "Of course we fight," Olivia told famed Hollywood columnist Louella Parsons. "What sisters don't battle? (Good question, Olivia!)

Apparently, the Fontaine/de Havilland sisters were at such odds that they couldn't even agree to share the same last name.

Olivia was the first to break into acting but copycat Joan followed shortly thereafter.

In 1941, the sisters were both nominated for Best Actress Oscars, Joan for her role in *Suspicion*, Olivia for *Hold Back the Dawn*. Hollywood gossip mills worked overtime churning out stories about sibling rivalry. On the night of the Academy Award presentations, Olivia and Joan were seated next to each other at the same table. (This was probably not their decision.)

Ginger Rogers presented the award for Best Actress that year. Tension mounted as Ginger read the nominees. All eyes were focused on the sisters. Then Ginger announced that the younger sister, Joan, had won the Oscar.

Spectators reported that, at the mention of her name, Joan froze and was unable to move. She was rescued by her concerned sister.

"Get up there," Olivia hissed.

Joan sprang to her feet.

Recalling the sensation of winning and her thoughts while walking to the dais to collect her Oscar, Joan told a reporter: "All the animus[1] we'd felt toward each other as children, the hair-pulling, the savage wrestling matches, the time Olivia fractured my collar bone, all came rushing back in kaleidoscopic imagery."

As she accepted her award, Joan cried. Perhaps she was remembering the broken collar bone. (Reportedly, Ginger cried, too.)

---

[1]Joan uses this word "animus." I don't know what it means either.

Back at the table, Olivia smiled faintly and shook Joan's hand. Later, she was overheard telling friends: "If *Suspicion* had been delayed just a little, it wouldn't have gotten in under the wire for this year's Award, and I might have won. . . ."

Five years later, in 1945, Olivia got her revenge when she won her first Oscar for her role in *To Each His Own*. Sister Joan rushed backstage to offer her congratulations. Olivia saw Joan coming and abruptly turned away. "I don't know why she does that," Olivia complained to her press agent, Henry Rogers, "she knows how I feel."

After the snubbing, according to *Daily Variety*, ". . . Joan stood there looking after Olivia with a bewildered expression and then shrugged her shoulders and walked off." When asked to pose with her sister, Joan curtly replied, "Really I can't. I haven't got time."

Olivia told a reporter, "Our relations have been strained for some time."

Press agent Rogers said: "The girls haven't spoken to each other in four months. This goes back for years and years, ever since they were children. They just don't have a great deal in common."

Their relationship improved slightly after Olivia married Pierre Galante, the editor of *Paris Match*, in 1955 and moved to France to live. Even though she eventually separated from Pierre, Olivia remained in France. Married four times, sister Joan has always lived in New York.

Psychologists often use the story of Olivia de Havilland and Joan Fontaine to point out that sisters can develop a better relationship if they follow the example of these two great actresses and live 3,000 miles apart.

Fourteen Surefire Ways to Drive Your Adult Sister Crazy

1) Tell her, "You're just like Mom."
2) Forget her birthday.
3) Remind her of the time she split her pants on the ski slope, didn't get invited to the Spring Dance, flunked algebra, got stood up, etc. This is particularly effective if you tell her these things in mixed company: say, when her handsome new boyfriend arrives for his first dinner with the family, during a cocktail party for her boss, or in front of her children.
4) Remind her of all the rotten things she did to you when you were kids.
5) Have a best friend.
6) Marry a man she can't stand.
7) After you've been in therapy for years and your sister wants to know what you tell your shrink about *her*, say: "Actually I don't think I've ever mentioned you." Smile sweetly.
8) Dress better than she does.
9) Lose weight.
10) Get a big promotion at work and make her take you out to celebrate.
11) Brag about your great sex life.
12) Wear expensive shoes.
13) Have perfect hair.
14) Borrow the family heirlooms (silverware, diamond necklace, grandmother's lace tablecloth) and keep them.

Sisterhood in the Workplace: The Old Girl Network

In 1970, feminist Robin Morgan wrote, "Sisterhood is powerful" and thereby created a whole new kind of sibling anxiety. As soon as the word "sisterhood" became a common buzzword among women, everyone began experimenting with the idea of treating all of their women friends as sisters. Women quickly learned this was a big mistake. Who needed yet another person borrowing money or vying for attention from loved ones?

Today, of course, the term sisterhood is as obsolete as 8-track tapes. In the 1990s, a more apt expression would be: Every Yuppie for Herself. Instead of treating our friends as sisters, we tend to treat them as co-workers.

Taking Over the Family Business

Sometimes blood sisters are forced to work together when they inherit a family business. A case in point was dramatized by William Shakespeare in his play *King Lear*. In this play, Shakespeare demonstrates an astonishing knowledge of sibling relationships.

King Lear had three daughters, a trio of sisters named Regan, Goneril, and Cordelia. They fought like cats and dogs. Shakespeare knew that, in many families with three siblings, two will side together, leaving the third child out. One child is always more prominent, eliciting strong feelings of love or hatred and the Lear family was no exception to this rule. In this play, Shakespeare has Regan and Goneril ganging up on Cordelia, a goody-two-shoes like you wouldn't believe.

After Lear stresses out to the max (this was before the

invention of Valium) Regan and Goneril try to take over the kingdom, but being typical First Born and Middle Child (i.e., bossy and uncooperative), they couldn't agree on operational procedures and, eventually, lost control to a bunch of corporate raiders led by Little Miss Cordelia. Shakespeare presented Regan and Goneril as two of the most selfish daughters a father could have, and of course, Cordelia could do no wrong, which was typical.

If Regan and Goneril were alive when Shakespeare was writing, you can bet your bottom dollar they would've slapped him with a law suit in two seconds flat.

Sister Separation

When two sisters grow up close in age, and in mind, there is a feeling that the two of them are like one. If nothing else, sisters often feel that it is them against the world.

At times, this is very comforting; at other times, it is stifling, especially when Mom insists on buying them matching winter coats every season.

Then there is the moment in time when sisters begin to realize that they are different people. This is called separating, and after this point, sisters usually choose wholly different life patterns.

Psychologists tell us that it's unusual to find adult sisters who actually work together or even share the same kind of career. "More typically, sisters choose diverging occupations in order to mitigate competition," says Dr. Franz Friedlander, head of the Psychiatry Sibling Studies Program in Point Pleasant, New Mexico, and a showoff with his vocabulary, if you want my opinion.

However, cases do exist where sisters overcome their differences and either share the same type of job or go into business together even without inheriting a company.

The Brontë sisters, for example, became writers and worked happily together at their home in England. The three girls—Emily, Charlotte, and Anne—all assumed male pseudonyms and spent their days and nights writing short stories, poems, diaries, and obscure magazines. They created their own private language, a world of characters and two of the greatest novels ever written: *Wuthering Heights* and *Jane Eyre*. Of course, the fact that the Brontës were all crazy as loons and compulsive maniacs to boot helped make their lifestyle possible.

A more recent case in point is that of Ann Landers and Abigail Van Buren, known in newspaper syndication as Dear Ann and Dear Abby. For almost thirty years, Ann or Abby or both of them have been named in the Gallup poll as the most admired women in America, in the *World Almanac* as among the most influential women in America, and in the *Ladies Home Journal* as among the one hundred most important women in America. Together, they are syndicated in over 2,000 newspapers and reach a reading audience of more than 200 million people.

Ann and Abby are identical twins, although plastic surgery has altered their identical appearance. Up until the age of twenty, they were inseparable; in fact, the first time they slept apart was on their wedding night. They were married in a double ceremony and honeymooned together as couples. Are they close?

"There was never a time we weren't speaking to each other," says Abby.

"There were some years we didn't speak," says Ann.

"I think being a twin is marvelous," says Abby.

"It's not easy being a twin," says Ann.

"If these are twin sisters, I'll take cobras," says Mort Phillips, Abby's husband.

Improving Your Relationship with Your Sister

As we have shown in previous chapters, sibling relationships are among the strongest, most potent in human development. Yet there are no religious rituals in the church or synagogue that acknowledge sibling bonds, there are no national holidays celebrating "Sister's Day," no gift-giving occasions, and, most important, no legal means to terminate the relationship. Much as you try, you can never legally divorce a sibling.

Consequently, you are stuck with this person *for life.*

Therefore, sisters need to know that their sibling relationships can be stabilized. First, sisters should understand that within the family structure, siblings are a kind of subsystem: not as important as parent-child but slightly more meaningful than parent-pet. Like most subsystems, though, the sibling relationship often breaks down and needs repairs that require great infusions of money, usually spent on a qualified therapist.

Sisters can improve their relationship by being more sensitive to each other's needs. To this end, we provide suggestions and areas to consider in trying to become a better and more helpful sister. These suggestions cost me about $25,000 in shrink bills but I offer them to you absolutely free of charge because, hey!, that's the kind of author I am.

Body Language

Communication between sisters breaks down into the following equation: 1% is verbal, 99% is nonverbal. In other words, *how* you talk to your sister is more meaningful than *what* you say to her.

Of course, you want to feel that, when you talk to your sister, you have her complete, undivided attention. How can you tell if your sister isn't listening? Check for these telltale symptoms.

When you are revealing the most intimate details of your personal life to your sister:

1) Do her eyes wander all around the room?
2) Does she fidget and/or stare at her nails?
3) Does she make a phone call?

Once you have your sister's attention, notice the messages being sent out by her body language. Gestures can convey a sister's true feelings. She could be saying something perfectly sweet and nice such as, "My, that's a lovely blouse you're wearing," but this comment is negated if, *at the same time*, your sister performs one of the following motions:

1) Crosses arms and raises eyebrows.
2) Crosses eyes and raises arms.
3) Holds up cross and spits on the floor three times.

Genuine Honesty

We all want to think that our sibling relationship is based on total honesty. On the other hand, most times sisters feel free enough to express their real feelings, and as any sibling knows, honesty can often be not only painful but vicious as well. For example, if you were feeling blue, how would your sister express her concern about you? Which questions would your sister be most likely to ask:

1) "Gee, is something bothering you?"
2) "Do you want to go somewhere and talk?"
3) "You look terrible! Why don't you do something with your hair?"

If you were feeling self-conscious about a new outfit and wanted your sister's opinion, would you expect her to say:

1) "That color really flatters you!"
2) "Try a bright scarf around your neck. Here, I'll lend you these earrings."
3) "Have you gained weight recently? You look as big as a house!"

Sisters should note the words they use with each other and remember that a small dose of honesty goes a long way, especially in the 1990s. "I don't want my sister to be a phony," said the 34-year-old waitress at my Greek coffee shop, "but I wouldn't mind if she lied a little."

Exercises for a Better Sibling Relationship

Here's a question psychologists have long pondered: Why do we save keys long after we've lost (or moved away from) the locks to which they belong?

The answer is because keys symbolize solutions and solutions are hard to come by.

It's like life. As adults, we are left with a box full of assorted solutions even though we no longer know the problems to which they belong.

To sort out the complexities of your relationship with your sister, try these helpful exercises.

One: Imagine the perfect relationship between you and your sister. How old are you? Where do you live? What are you wearing?

Remember that it is not constructive to indulge in the fantasy that you are an only child.

Two: Describe your sister as she would describe herself and have her do the same for you.

How closely do your descriptions match? Are you on the same planet?

Three: If all else fails, call Mom and start to cry. Your sister will be bound to catch hell.

Tips and Advice

Being a sensitive and caring sibling is not just a sometime endeavor, it's a full-time job. To be done well, the job requires certain skills and a real effort on your part. You can do it by following these helpful suggestions:

1) Keep your expectations realistic. Your sister will never lend you that turquoise dress with the seed pearls. So quit asking.

2) Be descriptive, not judgmental, when discussing your sister's husband, lover, significant other, or live-in boyfriend. Sure, he's a creep and you don't understand what your sister sees in him. Be nice anyway. Offer him a beer. Smile politely. Thank your lucky stars that you don't have to sleep with him.

3) If your sister starts to discuss something that really bothers her, reply by targeting the specific problem and not her entire personality. For example, if she talks about financial difficulties, discuss the possibility of getting a raise or doing freelance work. This is called effective criticism. Do not say, "You're so insecure. When are you going to grow up? And, it would be nice if you'd call Mom once in a while."

4) Avoid areas of conflict. Discuss only topics that you can agree upon. Avoid subjects that are unsolvable such as the way your sister drives a car, combs her hair, or disciplines her children. Acceptable topics: the latest episode of *thirtysomething* and Cher's love life. Agree to discuss only subjects that have been featured in *People*.

5) When you disagree, the one who started the fight and cries the hardest gets her way, but she must also have Mom over for the weekend. When all else fails, fight it out until one of you cries, "Uncle." In the event of a tie, both sisters must go to their respective kitchens and neither is allowed to watch television for a week.

6) Learn to listen. Adjust to your sister's style of communication, even if that means whining a lot. While she is talking, paraphrase her comments or say things like, "How interesting!" "How exciting!" or "Go on!"

   Tip: Wait till her talking comes to a full stop before offering your comments, advice, and criticisms. While she speaks, don't sit on the edge of your chair, shaking your head frantically and waving your hand in the air, impatiently waiting to interrupt her.

7) Like any important task, the proper tools help get the job done right. So, too, it's imperative to use the proper tools for improving communication among sisters:

   a) Directness.
   b) Kindness.
   c) Giving advice, not opinions.
   d) Cuisinart.
   e) Blood that is thicker than water.
   f) Airplane tickets to Hawaii.
   g) Call waiting.

8) Avoid the labels of your childhood. Don't think of your sister as "The Brain" or "The Pretty One" or "Miss Fancy Pants." Those were the labels of your childhood but you are no longer a child. It's time to grow up and treat each other as adults. So stick to the only labels that have real meaning in adult life: Calvin Klein and Anne Klein II, for example.

9) When a woman marries, the expectation is that her sibling relationship will not change. This is totally unrealistic. Expect major upheavals and traumatic confrontations because, although we learn to cope, nobody likes change and even fewer people like their brother-in-law.

10) A woman in San Diego, the eldest of eleven siblings, gives the following advice when dealing with a jealous sister: "I have seven sisters and I can tell you that

the only thing that works when dealing with their jealousy is indifference. Never speak bad of her and never speak to her unless you absolutely have to. When you do, always dwell on what is going wrong in your life and seek her advice because she has it all together. You'll never get her to come around so get around her. I know it sucks, but it works."

11) Admit that you were wrong about something. Confession is good for the soul and your sister will be so flabbergasted that she won't be able to talk for days. In such a state, she'll probably forgive you just about anything.

12) Finally, decide to stop treating each other as sisters and start treating each other as friends.

EPILOGUE

On May 3, 1988, *The New York Times* reported that a forty-member medical team successfully separated sixteen-month-old twin girls joined at the back of the head. The operation took place at a hospital on the outskirts of Johannesburg, South Africa.

The sisters names were *Mpho* which means "a gift" and *Mphonyana* which means "less than a gift."